LIKE
IT
IS

LIKE IT IS

Arthur E. Thomas Interviews Leaders on Black America

EDITED BY
EMILY ROVETCH

E. P. Dutton · New York

For information contact: Elsevier-Dutton Publishing Co., Inc., 2 Park Avenue, New York, N.Y. 10016

Library of Congress Cataloging in Publication Data
Thomas, Arthur E.
    Like it is.

    CONTENTS: Maya Angelou.—Henry Aaron.—Louis Stokes.—[etc.]
    1.   Afro-Americans—Biography. 2.   Afro-Americans
—Social conditions. 3.   Afro-Americans—Civil
rights. I.   Rovetch, Emily. II.   Title.
E185.96.T46   920'.009296073 [B]   80-25676

ISBN: 0-525-93193-7 (cl)
        0-525-93194-5 (pa)

Published simultaneously in Canada by
Clarke, Irwin & Company Limited, Toronto and Vancouver

10 9 8 7 6 5 4 3 2 1

First Edition

CONTENTS

FOREWORD:
THE ORIGIN OF
LIKE IT IS

The interviews in this book were first conducted by Dr. Arthur E. Thomas, Central State University's Vice President for Academic Affairs, on his TV program, "Like It Is." They span a wide variety of ideas, opinions, and plans, but they have a common base. All speak to the need for personal commitment, personal responsibility, and individual action.

At Central State, historically a black university founded in 1887, we understand the need to cope with all dimensions of student development—education, attitude, and self-image. We deal with both the will and the way to improvement and achievement.

A key element in CSU's approach is a weekly convocation at which well-known speakers of high achievement address the university community about their own experience and about the black experience. Afterward, "Like It Is" is taped for national distribution. The program is now carried on educational TV in nearly forty major cities.

The convocations, the TV programs, and the pages of this book convey the many messages of Black America—anger, hope, aspiration, frustration, humor, achievement, vigor, and creativity. They measure in many ways the road blacks have traveled and the far way to go. The parents of today's CSU students were the children of the late 1930s and early 1940s, when only 7.5 percent of blacks finished high school. Seventy-five percent do today, compared with 85 percent for whites. In 1940, college enrollment for blacks was around 50,000, compared to over one million today. But as measured by the promise of America, blacks are still disproportionately out of work, out of money, and out of the upstream jobs.

The transformation of the role of blacks in society is a measure of the task that remains. This book provides the understanding that can be put to use by both blacks and whites to continue that transformation.

LIONEL H. NEWSOM
President, Central State University
Wilberforce, Ohio

ACKNOWLEDGMENTS

These interviews first appeared on the television program "Like It Is," a series produced by University Regional Broadcasting, Inc., in Dayton, Ohio. The Ohio Television Network Commission and the Ohio Program in the Humanities, together with Central State University, provided financial support for the series.

I would like to thank Dr. Lionel H. Newsom, President of Central State University, and Richard Austin, University Attorney.

Many scholars contributed to the success of the program. From Central State University, my thanks to Dr. William Amoaku, Associate Professor of Music, Dr. Jeffrey Crawford, Associate Professor of Philosophy, Dr. Lucy Hayden, Chairperson of the English Department, Dr. Joseph Lewis, Director of the Indispensable Skills Program and Associate Professor of History, and Dr. Rubin Weston, Chairman of the Department of History. From Wright State University, I would like to thank Dr. Eugene Cantelupe, Dean of the College of Liberal Arts, and Dr. Lillian Howard, Assistant Professor of English.

Also essential to the creation and production of "Like It Is" were Ms. Carolyn Wright, Director of the Bolinga Black Cultural Resource Center at Wright State University, and Ms. Dawn Jones, Research Assistant for "Like It Is."

Mrs. Blanche Mayo, Mrs. Rosia Parker and Mrs. Sylvia Kelley were invaluable assistants with both the television program and the book.

This book is dedicated to Black Women—with love, trust, respect, gratitude, and appreciation.

ARTHUR E. THOMAS

EDITOR'S NOTES

I am indebted to many people for their advice and assistance: Dr. Lucy Hayden, Chairperson of the English Department at Central State University, Ms. Blanche Mayo, Assistant to the Vice President for Academic Affairs at Central State University, Ms. S. Lindsay Craig of the Harvard Graduate School of Business Administration, Dr. Bernard Watson, Vice President for Academic Administration of Temple University, Dr. William A. Dupree, Area Director of the Cincinnati Public Schools, Dr. Arthur Jefferson, Superintendent of the Detroit Public Schools, Dr. Barbara Sizemore, Associate Professor of Black Studies at the University of Pittsburgh, and Dr. Robert L. Green, Dean of the College of Urban Development at Michigan State University.

The *Like It Is* student panel helped gear the Teachers' Guide to student concerns. The Teachers' Guide is a separate publication developed to aid in school and college use of *Like It Is*.

Special thanks go to Dr. Arthur E. Thomas whose continuing encouragement and invaluable suggestions were essential to the final result.

My love and thanks to my family, who have always been there when I've needed them.

EMILY ROVETCH

Introduction

I asked Nikki Giovanni about the future of blacks in America. "We have to decide where we want to be," she said. "What excites me about the black community is that we are an emotional people, that we do an awful lot from the heart."

I asked Benjamin Hooks about the conditions blacks face in America today. He said, "Yes, this country's had a racist history, there's no question about it. . . . But whether somebody wants to eliminate me has nothing to do with my will to live and survive. I intend to endure, and to try to help blacks endure. . . . We've got great intellectual power."

I asked Maya Angelou about our history. She replied, "The Africanisms are rife in American life. And I suggest that's one of the reasons we've survived. . . . I know that people who love freedom, not the word, not the form, but the content of freedom, have hard work to do."

Warmth. Strength. Intelligence. Responsibility. These qualities have helped blacks survive, and will help us meet the future head on. I have seen these qualities in the people who have appeared with me on the television program "Like It Is."

Here are the voices of black America: their interpretations of the past, their understanding of today, and their plans for the future.

I hope the views presented here will create better communication, both in the black community and between blacks and whites. We have graduated from accepting everything handed us: the resentment, the racism, and the limitations. We have graduated to a stage where, instead of accepting too much or too little, we can communicate. We can communicate the nature of the black community and the black situation. We can communicate the nature of black oppression, without dwelling on that alone. We can communicate the realization that we have to help ourselves, but that to do so we need cooperation.

It is critical for all of us to hear and compare the voices of today's leaders. Obviously the black community speaks with more than one voice, but in our many voices there is a unity of purpose. Yes, we have a variety of ideas—without them we would stagnate. Yes, we have a variety of plans—without them our future would be blocked. What is essential is that America *hear* these ideas and *understand* the plans.

To stand together in the black community, we need to know what we're standing behind.

We're standing behind knowledge. Knowledge is power. Let me give you an example. When I was directing a student rights center in Dayton, Ohio, a nine-year-old came to see me. He said, "Mr. Thomas, the teacher keeps messing with me and the next time the teacher messes with me, I am going to mess with the teacher." And I said, "No, you're not." So we made a plan. And we practiced and practiced, just as if we were practicing for the Christmas play. He went back to school, and he was ready. The teacher said, "Sit down and be quiet." He was silent for the next twenty minutes, then he raised his hand. The teacher said, "What do you want?" And he said, "Mrs. Jones, you have psychologically dehumanized me to the extent that I may never be able to adequately function again as a human being, and unless you refrain from treating me in such a manner, I may have no alternative but to take you to the United States District Court and charge you with a psychological tort—a mental injury— because if insensitive teachers like you continue to brutalize potentially brilliant individuals like me, you destroy my life's chances." And he sat down.

Mrs. Jones does not bother my man anymore. He learned that knowledge is power.

We're standing behind our heritage, our blackness. We need to speak out about being black. Too many of us are becoming frightened; we are becoming black Anglo-Saxons. Congressman Parren Mitchell defined black Anglo-Saxons in our interview:

The black Anglo-Saxon has come down through a series of definitions. At one time that person was called an Oreo cookie, black on the outside and white on the inside. Basically we're talking about people who simply don't know how to think from a black perspective . . . this is the person who's afraid to use the word "black." He might use "minority," but he's scared to use "black." This is the person who's afraid to use a phrase like "white oppression." In other words, the black Anglo-Saxon just closes his or her mind to the reality of the present black experience and the reality of the black legacy.

We have a proud heritage. In the following interviews, you'll hear about the strength and endurance of blacks; the beauty of our poetry, literature, and music; the creativity and intelligence of black inventors; the determination of the founders of black institutions; the courage of those who struggled to allow blacks to vote. We can't abandon that heritage just because some of us have reached a comfortable place in society. We're living in a world where ten million children, black and white, don't receive adequate health care. We're living in a country where the average black man dies seven years before the average white man, where a third of black families live below the poverty level as compared to less than a tenth of whites, where black unemployment is almost two and one-half times white unemployment, where less than one percent of all elected officials are black—and yet over 13 percent of the population in this country is black.

To understand what we face today and what we faced in the past, we must record our own history. Only then can we deal with ourselves in a fair manner. We haven't always been dealt with fairly. But for every move to erase a Paul Robeson from libraries and history books, to present a Congressman Adam Clayton Powell, Jr. merely as a playboy rather than as a brilliant legislator, to publicize only the heroes who gain whites' approval—for each of these obstructions, we need to come back with a stronger voice. How do we present our heroes, our leaders, our friends? In spite of the unity we built in the sixties, we became divided because we listened to those desiring to divide us. It's time to listen to our own people and to heal that division.

We're standing behind the need for action. In our interview, Jesse Jackson stresses the needs for blacks to be involved in the world: ". . . we must fight to be people in the world; not just black people, but people in the world who are black." Black leaders are really world leaders. If we solve the problems we're confronted with, we solve problems for everyone. We can deal with the problem of energy. We can deal with the problem of racism. We can deal with the problem of hunger.

Yes, we've been oppressed. In our history in this country, attempts have been made to dehumanize us and contain us. But as I tell students, if you're contained, don't accept your condition: Grab a crowbar and lift off the weights that are keeping you down. That crowbar may be education. It may be litigation. It may be a better knowledge of what we've survived and accomplished. It may be listening to the leaders in *Like It Is,* and acting on what they say.

That's what it all boils down to—action. This book is not just for information's sake, it's for action's sake. I hope the information in here will be used to change something that is wrong, to do something that is right, to influence everybody's life.

We need to tell it Like It Is. We need to tell the facts. We need to present our ideas. We need to express our opinions. We need to let everyone know the complexity of our situation, we need to understand the variety of options open to us, and we need to act on them.

With the help of Alvin Poussaint, Rosa Parks, Julian Bond, Benjamin Hooks, Jesse Jackson, Jerry Paul, Maya Angelou, Louis Stokes, Michele Wallace, Henry Aaron, Nikki Giovanni, and Parren Mitchell, we are telling it Like It Is.

ARTHUR E. THOMAS

LIKE
IT
IS

MAYA
ANGELOU

BIOGRAPHY
MAYA ANGELOU

Maya Angelou is an author, poet, actress, and producer. Her three-volume autobiography powerfully describes her background. Through the books, we see Maya Angelou, brought up in Stamps, Arkansas—an America that was "flesh real and swollen-belly poor," a town where segregation was so complete, "most black children didn't really, absolutely know what whites looked like." We see Maya Angelou, living in St. Louis, Los Angeles, San Francisco; having a son at sixteen; working at jobs running the gamut from Creole cook to nightclub dancer—by the time she was twenty. We learn of Maya Angelou, raised with a combination of solemn determination, books, love, gaiety, and knowledge. Her mother taught her: "People will take advantage of you if you let them. Especially Negro women. Everybody, his brother and his dog thinks he can walk a road in a colored woman's behind. But you remember this, now. Your mother raised you. You're full-grown. Let them catch it like they find it. If you haven't been trained at home to their liking tell them to get to stepping . . . stepping. But not on you."

Maya Angelou—a woman of warmth, strength, determination, and intelligence. Her personal portfolio includes a list of plays, films, records, television appearances, honors, and special awards. In addition to her best-selling autobiography, she is the author of three books of poetry, and numerous short stories and articles. She began acting in the 1950s in the European tour of *Porgy and Bess* and recently starred as Kunte Kinte's grandmother on *"Roots."* Her writing credits include the original screenplay and musical score for the film *Georgia, Georgia*. She has written and produced a TV series on African traditions in American life, was guest interviewer for the Public Broadcasting System program "Assignment America," and has recently produced a two-hour TV special. Ms. Angelou is on the Board of

Trustees of the American Film Institute, and is one of the few women members of the Director's Guild. The recipient of numerous honors and awards, including the 1975 *Ladies Home Journal* Woman of the Year Award in Communications, she holds honorary degrees from Smith College, Mills University, Laurence University, Wake Forest University, and Central State University. In the sixties, at the request of Dr. Martin Luther King, Jr., she became the northern coordinator for the Southern Christian Leadership Conference. She was appointed by President Carter to the Commission on International Women's Year.

INTERVIEW
MAYA ANGELOU

ARTHUR THOMAS: Beautiful, brilliant, fantastic black woman—
why does it make you almost want to cry, and sometimes
cry, when reviewers tell you that you're a natural writer?

MAYA ANGELOU: Well, because it costs so much to write well. It is
said that easy reading is damned hard writing, and of course
that's the other way around, too. Easy writing is awfully
hard going to read. But to make a poem or an article, a piece
of journalism, sing—so that the reader is not even aware that
he or she is reading—means that one goes to the work
constantly: polishing it, cleaning it up, editing, cutting out,
and then finally developing it into a piece that hopefully
sings. And then one shows it to an audience and a critic
says, "She's a natural writer." There's nothing natural about
it. It costs a lot.

THOMAS: There's a tremendous amount of work in writing.

ANGELOU: Hard work. It's hard work. I think everything is hard
work. Everything I've seen that one wants to excel in. I push
toward excellence. Always. I think that we've become a
country which accepts mediocrity, rudeness, crudeness,
coarseness—as the norm. We have stopped asking not only
for excellence from others, we've stopped demanding excellence from ourselves individually. Too many of us, that
is.

THOMAS: I know you have worked all day and sometimes more
than one day on just two lines.

ANGELOU: All day! I've worked on one poem six months. One
poem. Because, first, I never wanted to write dust-catching
masterpieces. And I'm happy that my work is required

4

reading at almost every university in this country, either the autobiographies or the poetry.

When I write a poem I try to find a rhythm. First, if I wanted to write a poem about today, and my experience in southern Ohio, just today, I would write everything I know about today: every picture I've seen, every person I've met, what I know about the new friends I've made, how my mother's responding to this trip, you, the car—I would write everything. That would take maybe fifteen pages. Now I might end up with four lines.

But then I find the rhythm. Everything in the universe, Art, has rhythm. The sun rises and sets. The moon rises and sets. The tides come in, they go out. Everything moves in rhythm. Just tangentially, I would like to say that when people say of black people, "You have rhythm," it is not an insult.

THOMAS: It's a compliment.

ANGELOU: It is a compliment. It means that you are close to the universe. So, I would look for the rhythm of this morning, of waking in the hotel lobby, of driving here. And I will find that maybe the rhythm changes, just like snapping your fingers. The rhythm is slow and simple, and then maybe it's faster, more complex; and then there's the audience, and then—it's marvelous! Exciting!

Then I start to work on the poem, and I will _pull_ it and _push_ it and _kick it_ and _kiss_ it, _hug_ it, everything. Until finally it reflects what this day has been.

It costs me. It might take me three months to write that poem. And it might end up being six lines.

This is one poem that took me six months to write. It's called "Letter to an Aspiring Junkie."

Let me hip you to the streets,
Jim,
Ain't nothing happening.

Maybe some tomorrows gone up in smoke,
raggedy preachers, telling a joke
to lonely, son-less old ladies' maids.

Nothing happening,
Nothing shakin', Jim.
A slough of young cats riding that
cold, white horse,
a grey old monkey on their back, of course
does rodeo tricks.

No haps, man.
No haps.
A worn-out pimp, with a space-age conk,
setting up some fool for a game of tonk,
or poker or
get 'em dead and alive.

The streets?
Climb into the streets man, like you climb
into the ass end of a lion.
Then it's fine.
It's a bug-a-loo and a shing-a-ling,
African dreams on a buck-and-a-wing and a prayer.
That's the streets man,
Nothing happening.

THOMAS: Why does the caged bird sing?*

ANGELOU: Why does the caged bird sing? I think that was a bit of
naiveté or braggadocio for me to say I _know_ why the caged
bird sings! Actually, I was copying a Paul Laurence Dunbar
poem, so it's all right.

---

*The first volume of Maya Angelou's autobiography is titled, I Know Why
the Caged Bird Sings (New York: Random House, 1969).

I believe that a free bird, to use the same analogy, floats down, gets the early worm, flies away, and mates. . . . But the bird that's in a cage stalks up and down, up and down, looking constantly out. Out. And he sings about freedom. Mr. Paul Laurence Dunbar says:

I know why the caged bird sings, ah me,
  When his wing is bruised and his bosom sore,—
When he beats his bars and he would be free;
It is not a carol of joy or glee,
  But a prayer that he sends from his heart's deep core,
  But a plea, that upward to Heaven he flings—
I know why the caged bird sings!

I know that the people who love freedom, not the word, not the form, but the content of freedom, have hard work to do. It's easy to throw off these, "I love freedom. Oh boy. I love it. Oh, I really admire it. I like it a lot." It's nice to say it. But to really love it means that you take all the weight, take on the responsibility, for the time you're taking up and the space you're occupying. That's what loving is about.

And you have to sing. You have to. The black people created the greatest music in the United States during the most horrifying of experiences—the experience of slavery. And in enduring atrocities that would break our hearts if we really, really started to look at them. And out of that time people created a music that is sung all over the world.

THOMAS: Describe for us what you would regard as some of the most meaningful experiences in your lifetime.

ANGELOU: The first, of course, is having my particular parents. I have a brilliant mother who is a constant inspiration to me. She just retired three or four months ago from the Merchant Marines. She is an able-bodied first-class seaman. Nineteen years ago when she was going to become a seaman, I called her and I said, "I want you to meet me halfway between

Los Angeles and San Francisco. Let's spend two or three days together. I'll furnish the Dewars."

And she said, "Oh, baby, I'm so glad to talk to you. I want to see you, because I'm going to sea."

I said, "You're going to _see_ what?"

She said, "No, no, I've decided to become a seaman."

I mean, she's a realtor, she's a surgical nurse. I said, "Why on earth?"

She said, "Because they told me they wouldn't let women in their union. And you know what I told them, baby? I told them, you want to bet?" She said, "I'll put my foot in that door until women of every color will walk over my foot, get in that door, get in that union and go to sea." And they call her now "The Mother of the Sea." There are white women, black women, Asian women, and Chicano women shipping out of San Francisco. So that was my first great break. She's been that way to me: an inspiration. I have the birth of my son, when I was sixteen—my son is my monument, if I had one!

THOMAS: Grandmothers are also very important to you.

ANGELOU: Older black women, they have me, and they know it. They're like children: They sense that I just melt. You know? And if I have the occasion to have a black woman work for me in any capacity, I do my best to get somebody young, because old people, I won't let them—if they're typing, I say, "Oh, I'll type that, you don't have to. Oh, no, ma'am, you sit down. Let me!" I honor, I respect, and I cherish old black women and old black men for their wisdom.

THOMAS: Our tradition, our elders and our church. Important institutions.

ANGELOU: Absolutely.

THOMAS: Acting in "Roots" as Kunte Kinte's grandmother must have had an impact on you, just as the magnificent role you

Kunte Kinte is born to Cicely Tyson (left) while grandmother, Maya Angelou, watches in opening segment of "Roots". *(Wide World Photos)*

played had a tremendous impact on the world. Tell us about "Roots".

ANGELOU: I was playing my own grandmother, actually! That was the way my grandmother was then.

Alex Haley asked me to play the role, and so did the producers. I did it because I wanted to direct two of those segments. I'm the first black female director in Hollywood. And I was very keen. I explained to Alex, and to the producers, that they wanted me because of my name. Which is fine. I worked very hard for this name. And if you can't be used, you're useless, you see? There are other actors, female actors, who could have done the same job, better, possibly; but, I said, if you want my name, I want to direct two of those segments. I want to be considered. So my name was in the hopper with everybody else's, and they finally became so pressed for time that they needed someone with more expertise. I don't believe that they ignored me. They gave me a fair shot. I did not have the expertise to move 150 pieces of production equipment. I just didn't know how to do it.

I'm now producing a two-hour movie for NBC. My budget is a million and a half, and it's the first time a black woman has been given that responsibility—or took it. I don't know which! But I think part of that did come from "Roots", from my insistence that I wanted to direct and I wanted to have an impact on Hollywood.

THOMAS: You'll do it well.

ANGELOU: I pray God.

THOMAS: I know you have some very strong feelings on the question of Africanisms in American life.

ANGELOU: I believe Africanisms are current in American life. Not just in black American life, but in American life. One sees it in dance, of course, it can't be denied. One hears it in music, it can't be denied. The European in the seventeenth and eighteenth centuries sang Elizabethan rounds. Their music was composed of very pure notes. African music has the flatted third and the flatted fifth. So we hear, now, European music sung, created in the United States, with that flatted third and fifth. Like Cole Porter music: "Bewitched, Bothered and Bewildered." That's African. There it is. In the music we can't deny it.

In the dance we can't deny it.

What is so proudly hailed as a southern part of gentility, which is southern hospitality, is an Africanism. It was not famous in Europe, and I didn't see it growing along the moss-covered swamps. It was offered by the African. White American southern women who, "Just can't hardly talk, I mean, just faint, I mean, I mean, oh, I'll just faint." So weak? I suggest that's an Africanism. The African mother, woman, slave knew she herself could not practice these actions and gestures of gentility. So she told the white woman, for whom she worked and who owned her, "A nice woman drops her voice. A nice woman talks very softly. A nice woman faints at any chance."

Now in Europe, even in the courts of Europe, in the seventeenth, eighteenth, and nineteenth centuries, the women didn't act like that. But in Africa today you can go down the streets, see a woman with a hundred pounds of yams on her head, long yams, fat yams; and she manages fine, just walking fine, and you start to buy some, she lifts this hundred pounds off her head, takes it down, you make your trade, then you say, "How are you today?" She says softly, "Oh, as for me, I could faint." Right? And you can see it at its source.

The Africanisms are rife in black American life. And I suggest that's one of the reasons we've survived.

THOMAS: You talk about the basic difference between the experiences of the black woman in America and the white woman in America.

ANGELOU: White women gave up something about a hundred years ago. At one point in the history of the United States, in the pioneer days, white women were equal to men. Whatever one feels about what they were doing, women actually built their own homes; defended themselves, their property, and their children; were able—had to, in fact—drag those wagons across. They were fantastic women.

But just before the turn of the century, they allowed themselves, en masse, to be put figuratively on a pedestal. During slavery they cuddled down in what Richards called their "pink slavery," and allowed slavery to murder the black woman's children. And there was no affinity, no friendship, no empathy.

The black woman, however, has continued to work, has

had to work, since 1619. She has had to become this phenomenal person. Now, with liberation, there is the first hope that black women and white women can become friends. Because only equals make friends. Only equals. Otherwise the relationship is unbalanced. There's paternalism, some sort of indulgence, tolerance. But equals make friends.

Now the black woman lives in a black community, right? Given that the white community may look down upon her, in the black community she is an important figure. She is important in the church. She keeps the church going, usually. Not she as the minister, but supporting the minister. She keeps it going. She in the community as the mother of the community, as the grandmother of the community, is very important. She is the teacher in the community.

So the people who are looking down upon her are whites. But they are not her brothers, her uncles, her sons, her nephews, her lovers, her fathers. The white woman, on the other hand, has been ignored and ridiculed by her brothers. Her uncles. Her lovers. So she needs, and desperately, to have a sense of identity, a sense of herself. And I support it. I want to be free to have a white woman friend who I know is as strong a woman as I am. You understand?

THOMAS: And she must be able to understand.

ANGELOU: Absolutely.

THOMAS: That's the key.

ANGELOU: Absolutely.

THOMAS: You have had tremendous experience with reading, reading, reading. Talk to us about reading.

ANGELOU: Well, the documents are there. In our institutions of higher education there are libraries. In our cities there are public libraries. And in those libraries are the documents which have recorded human thought for centuries. *For centuries.*

You can go to a library and pick up Terence. Terence, in 150 B.C., said, *"Homo sum; humani nil a me alienum puto." "I* am a human being. Nothing human can be alien to me." 150 B.C. He was an African slave, sold from the west coast of Africa to a Roman senator. The senator freed him, and he became the most popular playwright in Rome. And here in our libraries there are six of his plays which have come down to us, two thousand years old. This black man, not Roman, not born free, not white, said, "I am a human being. Nothing human can be alien to me."

Now if you go to the libraries and you find those things and you read, suddenly you are closer to being liberated than you can ever be. It is only an education that liberates. Education helps one to cease being intimidated by strange situations. Once you have it in your mind, you can go anywhere. You see? I encourage young people to read Shakespeare, Leroi Jones, Sonia Sanchez, Charles Dickens, Robespierre—in French—read. Read. Find that there is nothing that is not human, that if a human being can do the worst thing, it means too that a human being can do the greatest. He or she can actually dare to dream a great dream! And really create a masterpiece.

If a human being did it, then obviously I have that capability of doing it. And so do you.

THOMAS: Many authors have meant a great deal to you: Paul Laurence Dunbar and his dialect poetry, Alice Walker, James Baldwin. Do you ever see yourself as more in one school of writing than another, for example, the James Baldwin school of writing or the Richard Wright school? Or do you see yourself as doing something different altogether?

ANGELOU: Well, I tell you, there are two things. One is that all comparisons are odious. That's the first thing. The second is a little phrase that was written by Machiavelli in 1513. Machiavelli had been exiled by the pope, and in an attempt to brownnose his way back into the pope's good graces he wrote a slim volume which is called *The Prince*. That slim volume has become the basis for all foreign, internal, and colonial power. And the greatest thing he did out of it all is to create one phrase, and the phrase is more powerful, more lethal than the hydrogen bomb. The phrase is, "Separate and rule, divide and conquer." I will not be divided from Baldwin, or from Wright, or from Paul Laurence Dunbar, or Alice Walker—none of it. I belong to everybody.

I'll recite "And Still I Rise." This is the title poem of my new book. In all my work, I've tried to say it. In my life I've tried to say it. In my relationship with everybody I've tried to say it: And Still I Rise.

You may write me down in history
With your bitter, twisted lies,
You may trod me in the very dirt
But still, like dust, I'll rise.

Does my sassiness upset you?
Why are you beset with gloom?
'Cause I walk like I've got oil wells
Pumping in my living room.

Just like moons and like suns,
With the certainty of tides,
Just like hopes springing high,
Still I'll rise.

Did you want to see me broken?
Bowed head and lowered eyes?
Shoulders falling down like teardrops,
Weakened by my soulful cries.

Does my haughtiness offend you?
Don't you take it awful hard
'Cause I laugh like I've got gold mines
Diggin' in my own back yard.

You may shoot me with your words,
You may cut me with your eyes,
You may kill me with your hatefulness,
But still, like air, I'll rise.

Does my sexiness upset you?
Does it come as a surprise
That I dance like I've got diamonds
At the meeting of my thighs?

Out of the huts of history's shame
I rise
Up from a past that's rooted in pain
I rise
I'm a black ocean, leaping and wide,
Welling and swelling I bear in the tide.

Leaving behind nights of terror and fear
I rise
Into a daybreak that's wondrously clear
I rise
Bringing the gifts that my ancestors gave,
I am the dream and the hope of the slave.
I rise
I rise
I rise.

THOMAS: Thank you, Maya Angelou. Thank you for the love you
generate. Thank you for the courage you have. Thank you
for the example you set. Thank you for the magnificent black
woman that you are. Thank you for "Like It Is."

October 13, 1978

HENRY AARON

BIOGRAPHY
HENRY AARON

"Hammering Hank Aaron" has hit more home runs than anyone else in the history of major league baseball. On April 8, 1974, he hit his 715th home run, breaking the previous record set by Babe Ruth. George Plimpton describes home run number 712: "Bill Acree, who's the Braves' equipment manager, showed me the bat he hit it with . . . it was splintered *against* the grain, which he'd never seen before. Unbelievable power."*

Henry Louis (Hank) Aaron was born in Mobile, Alabama, on February 5, 1934. He grew up knowing he wanted to play professional baseball. As a junior in high school he joined the semiprofessional Mobile Black Bears. Soon after, he signed a $200-a-month contract with the barnstorming Indianapolis Clowns, an originally all-black team which had its origins in the Negro League. A scout from the Atlanta Braves came to watch the Clowns play a doubleheader in Buffalo. Aaron got seven hits out of nine, two of them home runs, and the Braves immediately offered an option to buy Aaron's contract from the Clowns for $10,000. The following year, Aaron was named Rookie of the Year. During the 1954 season he became a regular outfielder for the Braves.

Voted the Braves' most valuable player in 1954, 1955, 1957, 1959, and 1971, Aaron was named to the National League All-Star team sixteen times. The first player to make both 3,000 hits and over 500 home runs, he is also one of only five players to ever hit more than 30 homers and steal more than 30 bases in a season. In 1957 he hit the home run that won his team a world championship; that year his statistics included a .322 average, 44 home runs, 132 runs batted in, and 118 runs scored. In 1976

---

*George Plimpton, *One for the Record: The Inside Story of Hank Aaron's Chase for the Home-Run Record* (New York: Harper & Row Publishers, 1974), pp. 5–6.

Aaron's historic 715th home run was chosen as the Most Memorable Moment in Baseball History. He holds a career record of 755 home runs.

Henry Aaron's easygoing, slow-speaking style masks a tremendous amount of power. Pitcher Don Drysdale describes facing Aaron at bat:

> I always used to think that he had a lot of Stan Musial in his stance. From the pitcher's mound they both seem to *coil* at you. The only sensible thing—if you couldn't get the manager to let you skip a turn against him—was to mix the pitches and keep the ball low, and if you were pitching to spots, it was important to miss *bad*. If you missed *good*, and the ball got in his power alley, sometimes you were glad it went out of the park and was not banged up the middle.*

In 1975 Aaron played for the Milwaukee Brewers. At the end of the 1976 season he announced his retirement and went on to become the first black executive in baseball, as vice-president in charge of player development for the Atlanta Braves. He is also a partner in the Aaron-Burton Investment Company.

Aaron donates many hours to charities and is president emeritus of the non-profit organization No Greater Love. A recipient of the Encyclopaedia Britannica Achievement in Life award and the NAACP Springarn Medal, he was appointed to the President's Council on Physical Fitness and Sports in 1978.

---

*Ibid., p. 10.

INTERVIEW
HENRY AARON

ARTHUR THOMAS: Racism is still very much alive, Mr. Aaron. It's alive in sports and it's alive in people's attitudes toward athletes. You played baseball for twenty-three years. Now you are vice-president of player development for the Atlanta Braves, the only black vice-president in baseball. You and many other brothers have made great contributions, great sacrifices, but the game is almost like modern slavery. You hit the ball, you learn the game; but they don't want to use your brains, they only want to use your brawn. Do you feel that even if you hit a thousand home runs you would still be thought of as a black man first and a home run king second?

HENRY AARON: That's true. It is very lonely up there. I've been fighting and been telling people all along that we've been superstars on the baseball field, and ridden in the front of the bus for ten or fifteen years, but as soon as our careers are over then they slap us in the back of the bus again. I feel until you express yourself, until you tell people what you want, you're going to always be a secondary citizen. When we finish our careers as baseball players, we can't just keep quiet. We have to tell people what we want. We have to let people know we want to manage, and we have to let people know we want to be executives. Sometimes we are a little late expressing our views about this.

THOMAS: So in baseball, as in anything else related to our people, we have to adopt the Frederick Douglass philosophy: He who hits back the least gets hit the most.

AARON: I have always said that. About my tenth year in baseball, they asked me what I wanted to do for my career. I said I wanted to be in the front office and work with young people.

20

Hank Aaron watches the ball as he hits his 712th homerun. *(Wide World Photos)*

And, years later, I happened to get that position. But those positions are not going to become open for blacks until we let people know we want them. For example, ten or fifteen years ago when Ernie Banks and Willie Mays and I were at the height of our careers, Ernie Banks told me he wanted to manage. I said, "If you want to manage, let people know you want to manage right now. Because those doors will not be open to you unless you let people know what you want."

THOMAS: What kinds of letters did you get when you broke Babe Ruth's home run record?

AARON: Well, I wish I could repeat some of them. Mostly they were hate letters. In 1974, the year I hit my 715th home run, I received over 950,000 pieces of mail. At one point I could not open my mail at all. I was getting threatening letters every day, telling me they were going to kidnap my daughter, who was at Fisk University. "Leave money here . . . ."

THOMAS: Why were they going to kidnap your daughter?

AARON: Because I was going after Babe Ruth's record, and I was getting close.

THOMAS: Because you were black, they didn't want you to break his record?

AARON: That's right. I had to have a bodyguard with me at all times, like I was a political threat to the United States!

THOMAS: Doesn't that speak to the fact that racism is still very much alive in sports?

AARON: There is no question that it is still alive. Racism is still here.

THOMAS: What is your job as vice-president of player development?

AARON: I am in charge of the minor leagues. That means I am in charge of our Triple A, Double A, and A teams and two rookie teams. I am in charge of the managers, secretaries, and the instructors. I am in charge of about three hundred people. I put the instructors at the right level and I put the ball players in the right position, in the hope that they can move up through the levels and help the ball club in the major leagues.

THOMAS: How do white folks deal with you in your front office position? Do they just walk right by you to the second in command? Do they relate to you as the boss, or do they indirectly tell you, "Look, man, you're black and I have to tolerate you, but I don't want you to tell me what to do?"

AARON: As a black executive you have to always put your foot down, because many times they will walk right by your office until you tell them you're in charge. Until you do that, they're just going to continue to walk by you.

THOMAS: You're the only black executive in baseball. Frank Robinson had a crack at being a manager for a while, but his team didn't win, and so he's no longer managing. White managers lose games, make mistakes, and they move from one club to another club. If Frank Robinson had been white, wouldn't he still probably be managing somewhere, even if he lost some games?

AARON: There is no question about it. He certainly would be managing some ball club. He managed the Cleveland Indians for a year and a half—they gave him a bad ball club and all of a sudden they thought that he could win a championship with it. He did not win a championship and they dismissed him. It is time for the baseball establishment to let a black manager stay in a position for a while so that he can manage a ball club without being intimidated by the owner who says, "I've got to win."

THOMAS: Why have we had black managers and front office people in basketball but not in baseball?

AARON: I've been trying to fight this for a long time. I have asked the commissioner, I've talked to baseball owners, and I've tried to get an answer. Believe it or not, a few years ago they told me, "We can't hire a black because we can't fire him. The black communities will get all over us if we fire him." That's not true. I know a lot of people who have had jobs and been fired. So I don't know what the answer is.

THOMAS: How many black baseball players do we have in the majors?

AARON: Somewhere in the neighborhood of 100, 150.

THOMAS: If you had your own black development union and the brothers stepped down together and decided there would have to be a black manager, could that have some impact on whether or not a black manager would become a reality in baseball?*

AARON: I think so. Baseball people, and the commissioner himself, need to let them know that now is the time to have a black manager. You know, we don't even have a black third base coach. And we never have had one.

THOMAS: The third base coach has to be smarter than the first base coach?

AARON: That's right, just like quarterbacks. We can sit here and treat this thing like it is something to play with, but it is serious. Jackie Robinson broke into baseball some thirty or forty years ago, and in all that time there has never been a black third base coach. We have had coaches, but we have never had a black third base coach. And the reason for that, I am sure, is because the third base coach is the one who gets the sign from the manager and flashes it to the hitter. That's supposed to take intelligence. The first base coach, the only thing he has to do is pick up the batting helmet the batter throws down to run the bases. That's all.

---

*This interview was recorded on December 18, 1979. In August, 1980, Maury Wills, a black man, was named manager of the Seattle Mariners.

You look at the whole structure of baseball and you say, why aren't there men in the front office? When I took my position as vice-president of player development they said, "No way you can handle the people or the job." I haven't found anything complicated about it in three years.

We really have a long way to go, not only in baseball, but just as black people. So many of our people now think they have it made simply because they are making a few extra dollars and are riding around in a Mercedes, or have a big house. We still have a long way to go. We have to stop and look back. In Mississippi and Alabama, a lot of black people are starving.

THOMAS: *Ebony* magazine recently asked a football superstar to visit black colleges and inspire students to study and become a credit to their race, and the superstar reacted by saying, "I didn't go to any of these black schools, I didn't get my money from them, I don't care what they do and I have some endorsements to make, so get out of my way." *Ebony* has said that many successful blacks—athletes, stars, educators—forget their roots. Now here you are, the champ, and you talk about baseball, but you are also concerned about blacks dying earlier than whites, about black colleges and universities, about the NAACP. With the fame you have received, how do you maintain that kind of perspective?

AARON: I think back to when I grew up in Mobile, Alabama. There were eight of us, and I'll never forget some of the things that happened to me back then. My oldest brother was on his way to work early one morning when the police picked him up. They were looking for a peeping Tom some white woman had reported. I never will forget when the police brought him into the house and accused him of peeping in this white woman's window. Now, he was a responsible man. He had been working at the same job for about ten years. But just because he was on the street and because the police were looking for "some black," he was picked up. And I never will forget them marching him to this lady's house. All she had to do was say, "Yes, he was the one," and they would have sent him away for fifty years. Or hanged him.

All of these things are still going on. And I just don't want blacks to think they have it made. I want them to realize that although they may have five or six extra dollars in their pockets, there are some kids down in Mississippi or Alabama still suffering from that same racism my brother went through.

THOMAS: Do you think the press is hard on black athletes?

AARON: They're not hard on the black until the black starts talking. Then they get hard on him. I'm considered all right as long as I keep my mouth closed, but once I start telling the truth about the racism in baseball, I get labeled as militant. Any time you speak out you become militant. The press is not hard on the black ball player as long as he goes out there, hits the ball, slides home, says "Um hummm,"—if that's all he does, then he's considered all right.

THOMAS: But if he takes a political stand then he's in trouble?

AARON: They don't think he should do that.

THOMAS: They don't want you involved in politics even though they're immersed in politics.

AARON: That's right. In 1974 when I hit the home run in Cincinnati to tie Babe Ruth's record, someone asked me what I wanted, and I said, "Just a minute of silence for Dr. King." It was the anniversary of his death. They sent word back that they couldn't do that because they don't get into politics. But I saw the owners of the ball team walking down a tunnel with President Gerald Ford. And they say they don't get involved with politics!

THOMAS: Sports Illustrated recently published an article saying the percentage of blacks attending baseball games is declining. What is the reason for that?

AARON: *Sports Illustrated* said that in the early 1950s about 3 percent of all blacks attended baseball games. Now only one percent is going to baseball games. I think one reason for the decline is that many black parents say, "Why should my kids go into baseball when they have other things to do?" Because as a ball player you do well while you're playing the game, but when you're through playing you have nothing left. So parents say, "I'm going to train my kid to be a doctor, lawyer, physician—anything other than a baseball player, because there is no future in baseball. That's been done and it has been proven that once your career is over, that's it."

THOMAS: Does having fewer black fans coming to games affect the teams? In basketball, for instance, some people have speculated that the white community is reacting negatively to seeing so many blacks on the court. They say it is hurting the gate. Do you think when white folks see too many black superstars on the team, they tell the management either directly or indirectly to get rid of those colored folks?

AARON: I believe that is true. Take the case of the Boston Celtics. Last year they went all out to sign Larry Bird of Indiana State. He is what they call a superstar, a white superstar. And I read in the columns the other day that they drew something like 15,000 fans to their basketball games. They are saying, the blacks are not coming to the games so we'll find some white superstar to play the game and bring the whites back to the games.

THOMAS: Are black superstars treated differently from white superstars by the team, by the public, or by the management?

AARON: The difference is this: When a white player reaches a certain status and is making a lot of money, he has all kinds of people coming to him and giving him the right kind of advice on how he should invest his money. We don't have that kind of training. We have to make it the best way we can.

The white superstar is treated better. The white superstar always gets the commercial.

THOMAS: Pete Rose says, would you rather see him or Dave Parker bite into a candy bar. How do you relate to that?

AARON: It is sad when you can read in the newspaper about things like this. Of course, what Pete was saying is not how he feels himself, but how companies in general feel about black and white athletes. If two athletes are competing for a chance to do an advertisement, a company will take a white over a black.

I hit over 755 home runs and the only big commercial I ever had was with Magnavox. It made me a lot of money. But that was the only one. I can remember when Mickey Mantle and Roger Maris hit that many home runs between the two of them, and they had all kinds of endorsements.

THOMAS: What would you tell young black ball players coming up today? If they have to decide between college and baseball, which should they pick?

AARON: I would hope that a ball player can finish school. If he doesn't finish school right away and he wants to start playing baseball, play baseball; but he should be sure to go back later and get his education. But if something has to go, let the sports go.

THOMAS: A recent article said that if a youngster was not an All-American by the time he went to college, he should think seriously about leaving a sports career alone because his chances of becoming successful in a sport were very small. Do you think that is good advice?

AARON: That is very true. I'll give you the example of my own son, who is now playing football at Tennessee. When he was in high school he weighed close to two hundred pounds. He didn't have to use any finesse, he just used brute force. So naturally he was above the rest of the kids. He went to college and he started playing with kids who were a bit heavier and who were playing just as well as he could play. He is no more that big force that he was in high school. So now he has to start seriously thinking, can I play professional football? Can I make a career out of it, or should I go on to school and make a career out of academics?

THOMAS: Do you think that black youngsters pay more attention to sports than to academic affairs?

AARON: I think some of them do. And I tell all of them what I tell my son. The most important thing is to try to get as much out of your books as you can. So many of our black youngsters think that because they have college sports careers they are going to go into the pros and do as well there. If an athlete happens to make the pro team and breaks a leg, then he really doesn't have anything to fall back on. My advice to any of them, if they think they are going to make a career out of sports, is to make sure that they get their education first and then depend on sports second.

THOMAS: Mr. Aaron, we thank you very much for what you've done for all people. You're a magnificent person. Keep on doing what you're doing. Thanks for "Like It Is."

December 18, 1979

LOUIS STOKES

BIOGRAPHY
LOUIS STOKES

When Louis Stokes was running for the United States House of Representatives in 1968, he told voters in white suburbia not to ask him to explain why a lot of blacks were so angry. "Angry blacks are here. They exist. There's no explaining them away. You get rid of the conditions that breed the anger and then you won't see so many angry blacks around."*

Congressman Stokes, the first black man to represent a district of Ohio in the House of Representatives, works to improve the situation of blacks by legislative means. He is currently serving his sixth term in Congress. As a black congressman he represents not only the people in his own congressional district, he also serves as congressman-at-large for black people across America.

In his second term of office, Stokes was the first black member ever to sit on the powerful House Appropriations Committee. He serves on the House Budget Committee, and is chairman of the committee's Task Force on Community and Health Resources. A past chairman of the Congressional Black Caucus, which lobbies for legislation speaking to the needs of blacks, he is presently cochairman of the caucus' Health Brain Trust.

The following interview focuses on the conclusions of the House Select Committee on Assassinations, which examined the assassinations of Dr. Martin Luther King, Jr. and President John F. Kennedy. Congressman Stokes was chairman of the committee. On December 31, 1978, he completed the investigations and filed with the House of Representatives twenty-seven volumes of hearings, a final report, and recommendations for administrative and legislative reform.

Stokes was fatherless by the age of three. His mother worked as a domestic to support her two sons, Louis and Carl. (Carl

---

*"New Faces in Congress," Ebony (February, 1969), p. 64.

Stokes, lawyer and former journalist and news commentator on NBC-TV, New York, made history in Cleveland in 1967 by becoming the first black mayor of a major American city.) Louis shined shoes, and was a salesman in an Army-Navy surplus store before he joined the army at the age of twenty-one. He attended Case Western Reserve University on the GI bill, and received his law degree from Cleveland-Marshall Law School.

Stokes did not at first consider himself a political man; his work was in criminal law. He built up a reputation as a defender of the black poor, fighting for those arrested in antidiscrimination marches and school board sit-ins. Although not an advocate of militancy himself, he represented militant black nationalists in court. When clients couldn't afford to pay him, he defended them for free.

It was through a court case that Stokes was persuaded to run for Congress. *Ebony* magazine describes the case:

> The Ohio Legislature in 1965 redrew the boundaries of the state's 21st district so that black wards were dispersed and black voter strength so diluted that a black congressional candidate would find it virtually impossible to win. Stokes was the attorney in a suit brought by black Republican leader Charles P. Lucas. He won the suit on appeal to the U.S. Supreme Court and saw the Legislature forced to backtrack, and come up with a new, acceptable redistricting plan in which the black electorate [was] 65 percent.*

Intelligence, compassion, and hard work characterize Stokes's fight for black people. Through his work in Congress he tries to achieve measurable improvements for his constituency, both in his district and across America, by putting laws on the books and putting those laws into action.

---

*Ibid., p. 60.

INTERVIEW
LOUIS B. STOKES

ARTHUR THOMAS: Congressman Stokes, when Dr. Martin Luther King was shot, is it true that one FBI agent said, "I hope they killed him"? And when it was learned that Martin Luther King was dead, is it true that the FBI agent said, "I'm _glad_ they killed the s.o.b."?

LOUIS STOKES: This is the testimony received by our committee. An ex-FBI agent by the name of Arthur Murtaugh, who had been an agent for twenty years, told our committee that when the radio broadcast came through in the Atlanta field office that Dr. King had been shot, the agent with whom he was leaving the office made the statement, "They got Zorro. They got the s.o.b. I hope he's dead." A few moments later when the radio stated that Dr. King was dead, Murtaugh told us that the man literally jumped with joy.

THOMAS: He jumped with joy?

STOKES: Correct.

THOMAS: Congressman Stokes, as a black man, knowing the tremendous contributions that Dr. Martin Luther King had made to the black people of the world, how were you able to maintain your objectivity and your scholarly approach throughout the hearing, knowing that a white man, a member of the FBI—is he still an FBI man?

STOKES: He's still a member of the FBI.

THOMAS: He may arrest some black person out there right now, with that racist attitude. Is anything being done about that?

STOKES: There have been changes in the bureau since then.

THOMAS: I'm talking about that man, though.

STOKES: He's still an FBI agent. Still serving with the agency today. And still as prejudiced as ever. We live in a racist society—a society that institutionalized racism. There are many duplicates of that particular agent throughout American society.

THOMAS: Do black reporters ever ask you if it was worth the money to investigate the murders of Dr. Martin Luther King and John F. Kennedy?

STOKES: Well, I can't recall having any black reporter asking me that particular question.

THOMAS: Do nonblack reporters ever ask you that question?

STOKES: Oh, yes, I've been asked the question quite a few times. I have spent $5.3 million. I am asked, in light of the conclusions of my committee, do I think it was really worth the expense. My reply is that I don't know the dollar value of a human life. I don't know the dollar value of the life of a President of the United States, nor do I know the dollar value of a Nobel Peace Prize winner's life, particularly when he happens to be probably the greatest black man that walked the earth. I then say to them that I don't personally care how many millions of dollars it cost. The dignity of these men's lives demands that their deaths be investigated, demands that we try to find who unlawfully and illegally took it into their own hands to take their lives.

THOMAS: What did the committee conclude?

STOKES: We concluded that in both the assassination of President Kennedy and the assassination of Dr. Martin Luther King there were conspiracies. We also concluded that Lee Harvey Oswald did in fact assassinate President Kennedy, and that James Earl Ray did in fact assassinate Dr. Martin Luther King.

THOMAS: Who else was involved in this conspiracy?

STOKES: In the King case we uncovered the outlines of a conspiracy that was based in St. Louis. A man by the name of Byers
revealed to an FBI informant that in 1967 he had been
offered $50,000 to kill Dr. King. The informant gave the FBI
the information in 1974. The FBI promptly misfiled it. But
they turned the misfiled information over to us in 1978, and
we pursued it intensively. This formed the basis for what we
feel is the conspiracy that James Earl Ray joined.

In the Kennedy assassination, we developed evidence
that there was another gunman on the grassy knoll in Dealey
Plaza. The committee was unable to ascertain who the
individual was, but we heard testimony presenting acousti-
cal evidence that scientifically established, beyond a reason-
able doubt, there was another shooter on the grassy knoll.

THOMAS: How many staff individuals did you have involved in
the investigation?

STOKES: A total of 115.

THOMAS: Out of 115, how many were black?

STOKES: We had probably the largest number of black employees
of any congressional committee in the House of Representatives. Usually, we are told that it's difficult to find
qualified blacks. I had my chief counsel go all over the
United States and recruit nothing but qualified blacks, both
black women and black men. I found qualified researchers,
qualified attorneys, and qualified investigators. In fact, the
two top investigators who headed up the investigation team
on the Kennedy and King assassinations were black: two
homicide detectives in the New York Police Department,
acknowledged to be the top detectives in the country, each
of whom had over twenty years' experience. We hired both
of them.

THOMAS: We spoke before of the racist attitude of an individual

Members of the House Assassinations Committee: Chairman Louis Stokes (D.-Ohio) (center); Richardson Prever (D.-N.C.) (left); Walter Fauntroy (D.-Washington, D.C.) (right) discuss Dr. Martin Luther King, Jr.'s murder probe. *(Wide World Photos)*

FBI agent. Could you describe any of the actions taken by the FBI as an agency which demonstrate the same attitude?

STOKES: The Cointelpro Operation, which was conducted by the Domestic Intelligence Division of the FBI, was an all-out war against Dr. King. That was the way it was described by Mr. Sullivan, who was in charge of the operation. And, of course, it had the blessings of J. Edgar Hoover, director of the FBI at the time, who had made the statement, publicly, that Dr. Martin Luther King was the most notorious liar in the world. As a consequence of putting this program into operation, the FBI put electronic surveillance on Dr. King, put physical surveillance on him; he was photographed and observed everywhere he went. Over five thousand recordings were made of conversations he had with other people, including conversations he had with his wife, members of his immediate family, and members of the Southern Christian Leadership Conference. The tapes were played to members of Congress to discredit Dr. King. They were played for heads of universities to stop them from giving him honorary degrees. They were played for people in the news media to get them to write derogatory articles about him. It was obscene and it was a gross abuse of both his constitutional and civil rights.

THOMAS: Is it true that when the FBI was working on discrediting Dr. Martin Luther King, they had already selected a man to be the new black leader who would do what they wanted him to do?

STOKES: Yes. The FBI assumed a lot of power when they set out to discredit Dr. King. They realized that, if they succeeded, they would be faced with the question of what to do with the Negro people. There were long discussions on the question in the documents we uncovered. The Negro people would be leaderless, and there'd be a void, and at that point in time there would be difficulties if the FBI didn't prepare to have someone else to lead them.

With that kind of arrogance, a total disregard for the rights of a whole race of people, they then came up with the name of a New York City black attorney whom they felt would be the "proper," as they put it, Negro to lead the Negro people.

THOMAS: Why did the committee determine that the FBI was not involved in the conspiracy to assassinate Dr. King?

STOKES: One of the things that I said from the moment I became chairman of that committee was that we were going to tell the American people what the real facts were. If I found that the FBI was involved in his death, I'd tell the American people that. If we found that they were not involved, we'd be honest, and tell the American people that.

What the FBI did was to create a climate through their actions that perhaps led other people to believe that they could with complete immunity or impunity kill Dr. Martin Luther King. To that degree the FBI had some responsibility because it did create that kind of atmosphere in this country—particularly Hoover, whose views were known by right-wing extremists. But in the actual firing of the gun and actual assassination, they did not do it.

THOMAS: Mark Lane says that a Memphis sergeant who was supposed to be guarding Dr. Martin Luther King, Jr. was temporarily taken away, and that was supposed to be part of the FBI's involvement. You went through a very intense investigation there. What were your findings?

STOKES: Ed Redditt, the black police sergeant, contended that he was security for Dr. Martin Luther King in Memphis. If he had actually been pulled off so that Dr. King could be assassinated, this of course had serious implications. We went into it in depth. Redditt had appeared before our committee in executive session and contended the story was true. But the committee continued to hammer away. Eventually, he broke down and admitted the whole story. He had been pulled off, it's true. But when he was pulled off, he was pulled off surveillance on Dr. King. And he just could not, as a black man, bring himself to admit to black people that he was spying on Dr. King. Ultimately, to his credit, he did appear in our open hearings, and he did admit publicly that he was not security for Dr. King. He was actually spying on Dr. King for the police.

THOMAS: During the hearings you produced a dated laundry ticket which forced James Earl Ray to admit his guilt. How did you do that masterful investigation job on the laundry ticket?

STOKES: Well, you know, I conducted the cross-examination on James Earl Ray. I spent a lot of time preparing for that cross-examination—you have to if you're going to do a good job as a lawyer. My background, of course, was criminal trial work. I knew everything you could know about James Earl Ray. I knew every bit of the evidence. I knew that he would probably try to deny that he was in Atlanta on April first,* because I had been able to establish that he had stalked Dr. King all the way from Los Angeles, California, to Selma, Alabama, over to Atlanta on April first. So, what he did was to put himself on what he called a slow trip through Mississippi, and that is where he contended he was—in some small town in Mississippi on the day and the evening of April first. I confronted him with the fact that he was in Atlanta on April first, and he said, "If you can prove that I was in Atlanta on April first, I will just take the responsibility for the King case here on TV." That's when I said okay.

THOMAS: You laid it out there.

STOKES: I brought the laundry ticket out.

THOMAS: After assassinating Dr. King, James Earl Ray traveled from Los Angeles to Atlanta, to Canada, to England and to Portugal. Where and how did he get the money to do this? How did he get his passports? And who helped him?

STOKES: We searched all of his finances and the finances of every member of his family. We've been through bank accounts throughout the United States, safety deposit boxes, and all kinds of employment records. His total employment in a period of about a year and three months was in a restaurant in Winnetka, Illinois, where he earned about $664. Other than that, he had no employment.

Our investigation led us to believe that he financed himself mostly through robberies. We believe he was connected with a three-man bank robbery in Alton, Illinois, where his part of the $27,000 take would have been approximately $9,000. During that period of time he estimates

---

*King was in Atlanta on April 1, and was killed April 4, 1968, in Memphis.

he spent about $9,000. That estimate tallies with what he seems to have spent.

He had many aliases, and it was suspected by many people that he had some help from others up in Canada in arranging his passports. But we found the system of getting passports was such that he could do it by himself.

THOMAS: Congressman Stokes, tell us about some of the more difficult things that occurred behind the scenes in the investigation. What kind of problems did you encounter?

STOKES: Well, as you know, in order to do an investigation of this type, both in the Kennedy and the King matter, we had to get into a lot of classified CIA documents and FBI documents. It was important that this committee's work be done. Every other intelligence-type committee set up by the Congress had failed. The Intelligence Committee in the last Congress was never able to maneuver into the proper type of an arrangement with the CIA to get hold of a CIA document. We were the first to be able to arrange to get to see every document we wanted to see. Many times, there were things they didn't want to give up. But we let them know that we were going to see everything we wanted to see or else the agency was going to have trouble from the courts. Eventually, eventually, with the exception of one thing from the CIA, we saw everything we wanted to see.

THOMAS: Don't you think that the investigations were ten years too late? That if the investigation had started earlier the details would not have been so cold and the victory of knowing who really was responsible would have been much greater?

STOKES: Yes. It was extremely difficult trying to go back and unravel all the facts and circumstances around two murders, one of which had occurred fifteen years earlier, the other ten years earlier. In the interim period, witnesses had died, witnesses had disappeared, evidence had been destroyed. It was extremely difficult. Had the FBI, for instance, investigated the St. Louis conspiracy in 1974 when they learned of it, obviously they could have unraveled much more than we could when they turned it over to us, untouched, in 1978.

THOMAS: What do you feel was the reason behind Dr. King's assassination? Was it a warning to black people to "stay in your place" in this culture?

STOKES: When Dr. King was killed, he had turned to a new area. He had begun to wake up poor people in this country, not only poor black people but also poor white people. We're talking about the vast majority of America. And many of us believe that entering this dangerous area, waking up white people in addition to black people, might have had a great deal to do with his death.

THOMAS: How do you see the 1980s in relation to the civil rights movement of the 1960s?

STOKES: In the 1960s, we demonstrated in the streets, we rioted, we had sit-ins, we had all the kinds of actions necessary to try to prick the conscience of a racist nation. And of course, through the action and leadership of Dr. King, and Roy Wilkins, and Whitney Young, and the other leaders we had at that time, we were then able to get certain laws upon the books.

The seventies and the eighties have to be devoted to what I would call economic and political empowerment with reference to the laws already on the books. We have to try and get real, meaningful political and economic gains if we are to be able to measure our full strength in these areas.

THOMAS: Congressman Stokes, you have exhibited courage and brilliance in your pursuit of this task. You have excited in us a new commitment to adhere to the philosophy of Dr. Martin Luther King, Jr., and to make his dream come true. Thank you for "Like It Is."

January 16, 1978

ROSA
PARKS

ROSA PARKS

On December 1, 1955, Rosa Parks refused to give up her bus seat to a white man. That simple action was the catalyst for the Montgomery, Alabama, bus boycott, which abolished segregation on Montgomery's buses and launched Dr. Martin Luther King, Jr. as a national leader. Mrs. Parks is known as the "mother of the civil rights movement."

Rosa Louise Parks was born in Tuskegee, Alabama, on February 4, 1913. Her father was a carpenter, her mother a former school teacher. At fifteen she graduated from Booker T. Washington Junior High School. She then took courses at the Alabama State College for Negroes. She was a clerical worker and an insurance saleswoman before becoming a tailor's assistant. Rosa married Raymond A. Parks, a local barber, shortly before her twentieth birthday.

Mrs. Parks soon became involved in the black community, serving as secretary and youth advisor for the Montgomery NAACP, and working with the Montgomery Voters League to register blacks to vote—an uphill battle because of the tensions between blacks and whites in Montgomery.

These tensions were evident on the city buses, where, in the words of Dr. Martin Luther King:

> ... the Negro was daily reminded of the indignities of segregation. ... It was not uncommon to hear [the bus-drivers] referring to Negro passengers as "niggers," "black cows," and "black apes." Frequently Negroes paid their fares at the front door, and then were forced to get off and reboard the bus at the rear. Often the bus pulled off with the Negro's dime in the box before he had time to reach the rear door.
>
> An even more humiliating practice was the custom of forcing Negroes to stand over empty seats reserved for

"whites only." Even if the bus had no white passengers, and Negroes were packed throughout, they were prohibited from sitting in the first four seats (which held ten persons). But the practice went further. If white persons were already occupying all of their reserved seats and additional white people boarded the bus, Negroes sitting in the unreserved section immediately behind the whites were asked to stand so that the whites could be seated. If the Negroes refused to stand and move back, they were arrested.*

Mrs. Parks refused to stand and was arrested, but instead of paying court fines she appealed the case. Her arrest became a test case for the legality of segregation on buses.

In his book, *Stride Toward Freedom: The Montgomery Story*, Dr. King describes the events launched by the arrest of Mrs. Parks: the year-long black boycott of Montgomery's buses, cutting bus revenue by over 65 percent; the formation of a transportation system operated with military precision by the black community, allowing blacks to get around without buses; the national publicity resulting from the boycott; and the Supreme Court decision that ruled segregation on buses illegal, allowing blacks to sit in buses on a first-come, first-served basis.

Sparked by a calm refusal to move, blacks in Montgomery were able to change history. Dr. King expressed their commitment in a church meeting as the boycott began:

If you will protest courageously, and yet with dignity and Christian love, when the history books are written in future generations, the historians will have to pause and say, "There lived a great people—a black people—who injected new meaning and dignity into the veins of civilization." This is our challenge and our overwhelming responsibility.†

---

*Dr. Martin Luther King, Jr., *Stride Toward Freedom: The Montgomery Story* (New York: Harper & Brothers, Publishers, 1958), pp. 40–41.

†Ibid., p. 63.

INTERVIEW
ROSA PARKS

ARTHUR THOMAS: Mrs. Parks, what were you thinking about on December 1, 1955? What happened during the day?

ROSA PARKS: During the day, I was working in the men's alteration department of the Montgomery Fair Store, and it was leading up to the Christmas holidays. The work was quite heavy. I had to work alone that afternoon because the young man who was the tailor had opened up a shop for himself, and he decided that he was going to take some of his work there. At lunchtime I went to the office of Attorney Fred Gray and stopped a short while there.* I didn't have any thoughts of anything special happening that evening. But I noticed how discouraged he seemed to be because he had nothing special to do but just sit around the office, waiting for something to do. And I left and went back to the tailor shop and finished out the day. I was quite tired, of course. I had worked pressing pants, putting cuffs in the hems, and so on. I felt some nagging pain around the neck and shoulders, and I was just generally weary.

When I went out of the store to go home, I noticed the buses were quite crowded, and instead of trying to get on a bus that was already crowded, I decided to go to a drug-store nearby, where I had in mind buying an electric heating pad. I went over there, and I didn't see the pad I wanted, so I picked up another item or two and came back across the street to catch the bus.

As I saw the bus approach I noticed that there seemed to be some vacancies; I didn't notice anybody standing. But by the time I got to the bus there was a crowd of people getting

---

*Attorney Fred Gray represented Rosa Parks in court when she was tried for refusing to give up her bus seat.

on, and when I got in the bus there was no room in the back of the bus up to where we could sit. But there was one vacant seat. It was alongside a man, and two women were across the aisle. I was pretty glad to get this seat.

The bus went on from that stop. That was on Court Square, right by the center of Montgomery, downtown Montgomery. There were a few vacancies in the very front of the bus, in the white section. At the next stop a few people got on and there were no more vacancies. We got to the third stop and several white people got on, and one white man was standing, and the driver noticed him standing. Of course, the passenger himself didn't do anything but just find a place to stand. He didn't request a seat. But the driver didn't want to see this white person stand up, even though the back of the bus was just packed with black people standing all the way up to where I was sitting. He asked for us to let him have those front seats, the seats that the four of us were sitting in. No one stood immediately. Then he said, "You all better make it light on yourselves and give me those seats."

At this point the man next to the window in the seat with me stood up, and the two women across the aisle stood up, but I refused to stand. I made room for the man to pass by me and move out into the aisle, and then I sat next to the window. The driver asked me if I was going to stand, and I said, no, I wasn't. Then he said, "If you don't stand up, I'll call the police and have you arrested." I told him to go on and call them, and he got out of the bus. I could hear little undertones of talk between people, but I couldn't understand what they were saying. A few people requested a transfer to get another bus.

A short while later, the driver came back on the bus with two policemen. He pointed me out, and said that he "had to have those seats and the other three stood, but that one wouldn't." He didn't say three _what_, men or women, didn't refer to anything, just, "that one," pointing to me, "wouldn't stand up."

The policeman, the only one who spoke to me, and encouraged me, asked me if the driver had asked me to stand, and I said, "Yes, he did."

He said, "Well, why didn't you stand?"

I told him I didn't think I should have to stand up. I asked him, "Why do you all push us around?"

He said, "I don't know, but the law's the law, and you're under arrest."

As soon as he told me I was under arrest, I stood up. One of the policemen picked up my purse, and the other picked up my shopping bag, and we got off the bus. They escorted me to the police car, and I sat down in the back. Then they had to go back to the bus to find out whether the driver wanted to swear out a warrant or whether he just wanted to be rid of me and forget it there. But he insisted on swearing out the warrant and said he would sign it when he made this run to the end of the bus line and came back.

THOMAS: Why do you think, Mrs. Parks, he insisted on having you arrested?

PARKS: You'd have to ask him that! I suppose he just wanted to extend his power, because in the city ordinance the bus-drivers were given police power to rearrange seating on the buses in keeping with racial segregation. However, in my case, it was not a matter of rearranging the seating, it was a matter of depriving me and the others of the seats we had been permitted to occupy, because the driver didn't make any request for our seats until this one white man was on the bus as a passenger, and standing.

THOMAS: Mrs. Parks, twelve years before that time, you had shown a great deal of courage and had been evicted from a bus too, right?

PARKS: By the same driver who had me arrested.

THOMAS: What happened that time?

1955: Rosa Parks is arrested and fingerprinted for violating bus segregation laws. Her refusal to move to the back of the bus touched off the bus boycott. Montgomery, Alabama. (*Wide World Photos*)

PARKS: I had got on the bus. I was on my way from Maxwell Field Air Force Base, where I was working. That time again I was feeling quite ill. I was just exhausted. I got on the bus and it was practically vacant in front of me, but people were standing, just packed in the back of the bus. As I got on and gave the driver my transfer, he said, "Go and get in the back door."

I told him that I was already on the bus and I wasn't going to get off the bus and go around to the back to get in. He got up out of his seat, took me by the arm, and just escorted me off the bus. He was very abusive in his way of speaking to me. But I did get off the bus and had to wait until I could get another bus to go on.

THOMAS: And there had been times when, because of the way you felt they would treat you, you did not even ride the bus, but chose to walk.

PARKS: I walked a lot of times and tried to use other means of transportation—especially after the arrest of a young fifteen-year-old schoolgirl named Claudette Colvin, in March of 1955.* I rode the bus as little as I could from then on. But it happened that I was riding a bus on December 1 because it was late in the evening and quite dark, and I didn't have any other means of getting home unless I walked alone. The weather was chilly and I was tired, so I got on the bus.

There were a number of incidents of abuse that happened to people in Montgomery, physical abuse as well as verbal abuse.

THOMAS: You knew when you told that man you were not going to get out of your seat, that physical violence could have resulted, didn't you?

PARKS: Yes, I did. I didn't think too much about it at the beginning, but I was resigned to the fact that I had to express my unwillingness to be humiliated in this manner, by protesting, by refusing to stand up.

THOMAS: Before your arrest, you had been involved in activities for the National Association for the Advancement of Colored People for quite some time in Montgomery.

PARKS: Well, actually, I became a member of the Montgomery NAACP and was elected secretary in 1943. That was during World War II. My husband was, of course, a charter member

---

*Claudette Colvin was forcibly evicted, kicking and screaming, from a bus in Montgomery, after she refused to give up her seat to a white man. However, Miss Colvin's arrest was not the catalyst for the civil rights movement that Mrs. Parks's arrest was. Miss Colvin was not well-known and active in the black community, as Mrs. Parks was; also, she was charged with disorderly conduct and not violation of the municipal ordinance on bus seating.

of the NAACP some years back. He was involved in trying to encourage black people to become registered voters. He did not meet with much success because of the intimidation and indifference our people felt. At that time, in order for one of our people to be registered to vote they had to be vouched for and supported by a responsible white citizen, and there were not too many white people willing to come forward and sponsor or promote the registration of a black person to vote.

THOMAS: Did you work with young people in the NAACP?

PARKS: Yes, but it was very difficult. When I got a communication from the national office about setting up a Youth Council, I couldn't find enough parents who were willing to pay the membership to get a charter. We had to have twenty-five members to get a charter and set up an organization. It was a long and difficult problem, because at that time the NAACP was considered far too militant, or too radical, or too dangerous, and a few of the people who themselves participated and were members did not encourage young people to get involved. They felt the NAACP was too dangerous.

THOMAS: Your contribution has been tremendous and a lot of demands have been placed upon you. How has that affected your feelings? Has it been difficult? Would you rather not have had all of it happen?

PARKS: I am gratified that people have been interested enough to continue to ask these questions and to want me to appear and talk, and explain the past. It has been very taxing on me physically and mentally. When I was arrested, no other person stood and said, "If you put this woman in jail, I am going to . . ." I had the feeling of being very much alone, as though I had no friend at all. There were even people on the bus who knew me personally, and one man in particular would not even go by my house to tell my husband that I had been arrested. I mean, they just went on their way.

On the other hand, in later times people came up in mass to protest what had happened to one of us. I feel gratified that no longer would any of us stand by idle and watch someone taken off to jail, or whatever happened, and feel indifferent to it.

THOMAS: Was your action due to frustration with the circumstances at the time, or was it a deliberate, planned choice to overcome the Jim Crow laws?

PARKS: Both frustration and circumstances would play a part. Even though at that point I had no knowledge or even expected the community to take the action that it did, I still felt it was what I myself had to do in order to show my protest against being oppressed as a person.

THOMAS: Did you feel at the time that your refusal to move would be the spark to ignite the civil rights movement?

PARKS: I had no idea what it would spark, or what interest would generate from this. It was not that I got on the bus and permitted myself to be arrested because I thought anybody else would do anything at all. I was very grateful that they took this as an incentive to unify the pursuit to do away with segregation, and did not give up, and did not accept the thought of being oppressed.

THOMAS: But the leaders at that time seized the opportunity to use you as the vehicle for the movement because you had what they call impeccable character.

PARKS: I was just like anyone else. I had made my mistakes and had problems, too. At the time I was forty-two years old, married, a member of the church, working hard every day, and trying to work with the NAACP. There was not much I could do except struggle on. There were times when it would have been easy to fall apart or to go in the opposite direction, but somehow I felt that if I took one more step, someone would come along to join me.

THOMAS: Mrs. Parks, we love you, we trust you, we respect you, and we thank you from the bottom of our hearts, for "Like It Is."

May 11, 1979

BENJAMIN HOOKS

BIOGRAPHY
BENJAMIN HOOKS

On January 10, 1977, Benjamin L. Hooks was unanimously elected executive director of the National Association for the Advancement of Colored People. He assumed office on August 1 of that year. Mr. Hooks has injected new vitality into the traditional goals of the nation's largest and oldest civil rights organization. At one of his speaking engagements, this sense of action came through loud and clear:

> Black Americans are not defeated. The civil rights movement is not dead. If anyone thinks that we are going to stop agitating, they had better think again. If anyone thinks that we are going to stop litigating, they had better close the courts. If anyone thinks that we are not going to demonstrate and protest any misrepresentation of this [Baake] decision, they had better roll up the sidewalks . . .*

Born in Memphis, Tennessee, in 1925, Hooks was the fifth of seven children. He graduated from Tennessee's LeMoyne College, and during World War II served in Italy with the 92nd Infantry Division. Once back in the United States, Hooks earned a law degree at DePaul University in Chicago—at that time, Tennessee law schools did not accept blacks.

In the late 1940s, Hooks returned to the South and was ordained a Baptist minister. During the fifties and sixties he combined the professions of preacher, lawyer, and businessman. As a preacher, he is currently on leave from the Middle Baptist Church in Memphis, Tennessee, and the Greater New Mt. Moriah Baptist Church in Detroit, Michigan. As a lawyer, he was appointed an assistant public defender in Memphis, and

---

*L. Norment, "New Life for an Old Fight," Ebony (November, 1978), p. 83.

then a criminal court judge, the first black judge in the Shelby County Criminal Court. As a businessman, he was the cofounder and vice-president of the Mutual Federal Savings and Loan Association of Memphis. Hooks also found the time to produce and appear on local television programs, to serve on the board of Martin Luther King, Jr.'s Southern Christian Leadership Conference, and to participate in NAACP sit-ins.

In 1972 Hooks became the first black appointed to the Federal Communications Commission (FCC). His position that the FCC should favor minority participation in the ownership of broadcasting facilities was given the weight of the law by a federal court. Hooks still feels that communication is one of the most powerful tools blacks have with which to fight racism. "Until we become part of the image-making process," he says, "we are foredoomed to failure."*

Hooks left the FCC in 1977 to replace Roy Wilkins as the NAACP's executive director. He has been applauded for encouraging ideas and opinions from members of the NAACP, and for taking action when action is necessary. Traditionally, the NAACP has fought to combat racial hatred and poverty through demonstrations and litigation. Some of its strongest work has been in the areas of voter registration, civil rights laws, school desegregation, and job opportunities.

Under Hooks, the NAACP has launched a number of new social programs, and expanded several others. One new program is ACT-SO, the Afro-Academic Cultural Technological Scientific Olympics. The program encourages black youths to strive for excellence and academic achievement. Another program, Project Rebound, assists prison parolees in readjusting to society by helping them find employment and housing. The NAACP Communications Department, created in 1978, works to fight racism in communications.

Because of his wide-ranging, freewheeling addresses, which have been called a blend of university lecture and

---

*C. C. Douglas, "Watchdog of the Airwaves," Ebony (June, 1975), p. 60.

old-time Baptist sermon, Hooks is in great demand as a public speaker. He makes two or three speeches a week around the country. The pace is hectic, but Mr. Hooks realizes that the NAACP must increase its membership in order to increase its clout, and it must have clout to continue its work to achieve full equality for blacks.

INTERVIEW
BENJAMIN HOOKS

ARTHUR THOMAS: Mr. Hooks, about ten years ago Samuel Yette wrote a book titled *The Choice: The Issue of Black Survival in America*. He claimed that since there is no more cotton to pick and there are no more ditches to dig, blacks are no longer necessary to America. He said there is a deliberate attempt to eliminate us. Does that appear to be the case today?

BENJAMIN HOOKS: I don't know that I necessarily agree with Dr. Yette's major premise. Even if it were true, the fact that you might want to eliminate me has nothing to do with whether I'm going to let you do it or not. I have never concentrated, in the years I've been in the NAACP, in the years I've been in this world, on what the white folks wanted to do with me. I've concentrated on what I want to do for myself.

A lot of young blacks are crazy now. They've been brainwashed so much they don't believe in themselves; they don't believe in anything much, and everything is negative. I look back to the start of 1863 when black people were reputedly free, and yet all the accouterments of freedom had been denied them—they were denied the ability to read, to write; they were given no forty acres and a mule, no goverment programs. And I would suspect that if they had no more stick-to-it-iveness and perseverance than we have now, we would not have survived.

Yes, this country's had a racist history, there's no question about it. There are a lot of things that are wrong now, and we still have a long way to go. But whether somebody wants to eliminate me has nothing to do with my will to live and survive. I intend to endure, and to try to help other blacks to endure.

THOMAS: In many parts of our community there appears to be a feeling of despair and anguish, a disgusted attitude. People are giving up. What do you advise blacks to do in the face of Proposition 13, Bakkeism, and the other problems confronting us?

HOOKS: The despair is understandable. I've spent half my life fighting for the things the white man takes for granted. I've had to fight to prove that I could do things; whether I could or not was not important: I was perceived as though I couldn't. So it's no wonder to me that there's despair, and anguish, and hopelessness in the black community, when everything we try to do seems to be taken away from us. But I still maintain that essentially what happens to a man or woman is not a matter of exterior circumstances, but of internal force. In my youth there was no social security, no unemployment benefits, no old-age pension; there were no subsidies of any kind, no hot lunches or hot breakfasts, or anything else. The only thing the city provided if you ran out of money was a poorhouse. And yet there was amazing resilience in the black community, an ability to survive, a sense of family, a sense of relationship, a sense of belonging—an identity which did much to enable black folks to survive against the most hostile circumstances.

I do not perceive, by any stretch of the imagination, that Proposition 13, or Bakke, or the present conservative mood of the Congress is anywhere near as bad as was the Post-Reconstruction period starting in 1879.* I don't perceive that we have as many problems now as we did then. And I take comfort in the fact that our foreparents, with limited education and no money but with a faith in themselves and

---

*Reconstruction (approximately 1865–1877) was an attempt to set up state governments after the Civil War which would equalize black/white conditions. Through a series of bills, blacks were given the right to vote, hold office, and own land. However, during the Post-Reconstruction period, almost all of the rights which had been granted to blacks were taken away. The right to vote, for example, was counteracted by requiring blacks to take literacy tests, or to pay poll taxes.

in God, surmounted all obstacles. They did what it was said couldn't be done. They survived, endured, and passed on to us a great legacy.

THOMAS: Then your philosophy is, I cried because I had no shoes until I saw the man who had no feet.

HOOKS: Yes, that might be a good summing up of it.

THOMAS: As you travel the country, what do you tell college students who say, "Why should I invest in the NAACP? What has the NAACP done for me?"

HOOKS: I've talked with a lot of college students who've been turned off by the NAACP's reputation and philosophy as they understand it. The first thing that concerns me is they don't know what it is all about. And I'm a little irritated by people who reject me; it reminds me of what white folks have done. When I served on the Federal Communications Commission, they didn't look at my background as a lawyer, as a judge, as a community activist. They looked at the color of my skin. And they wanted to see, "What is this black man going to do?" I had to do something more than any white person ever had to do, because they pre-judged me. To the same extent that whites have judged us, many black people judge their own institutions. They have not studied or researched the works of James Weldon Johnson, W.E.B. DuBois, Walter White, or Roy Wilkins. They have not read the history of the NAACP. But they get some notion that it's not what they want it to be, so they resist it. Now let me hasten to add, *after* you read about the NAACP you may not like it, and I have no argument if people want to be a part of the National Urban League, PUSH (People United to Serve Humanity), or the SCLC (Southern Christian Leadership Conference). The thing that irritates me is for folks to be against everything and not for anything. If you're dis-satisfied with everything that's going on, then start your own movement.

You know, we've got great intellectual power. If you

look at the record, there are one million young black people today in postsecondary education. There are more black youngsters in college in America than there are English people in college in all of Great Britain, and there are 55 million English people in Great Britain, and only 25 million blacks in America. We have made tremendous progress in the field of education.

So I say three things to young people. First, become aware of your own history. Know what it is all about. Don't let anybody brainwash you into believing that we are dumb, that we have to always be dancing and scratching and blowing trumpets or tooting horns. We've got great intellectual power. Second, being aware of that, utilize your own. Study, get all your school has to offer, and use it in the best way you can. Third, be involved with programs that can help the nation go forward. If you're not satisfied with any existing institution, there's no law or barrier that will keep you from starting your own.

THOMAS: What is the NAACP's agenda for the eighties?

HOOKS: If I look on the back of my NAACP card and see the objectives adopted in 1909, I find we are still fighting to make those objectives come true. One of the biggest mistakes any black person can make is to assume that we now have it made, that the fight is over. The Harris poll about a year ago indicated that a majority of whites felt blacks had now caught up, that everything was hunky-dory and no more special programs were needed for blacks. I sometimes get the impression that a few blacks have been brainwashed like that.

We have as far to go as we've already come. We're fighting for political, economic, and social equality and opportunity. In my judgment it's going to be more and more difficult because of the economic situation now. On today's job market a white high school graduate still makes as much as a black college graduate. We still have a lily-white Senate. There are only seventeen blacks in the House of

Representatives. We don't have a single black serving as a governor in any of the fifty states. We have four thousand black elected officials—that's great. But that's less than one percent of all elected officials in this country.

Our agenda for the eighties is to continue to move to make black people first-class citizens in every sense of the word. We plan to do that through the historic time-honored methods we've used. I'm not trying to find something new. The National Organization of Women, the League of Women Voters, the American Civil Liberties Union, the gay rights movement—they're all using methods the NAACP has used, and used very successfully. And yet folks come to me and say, "What new things are you going to do?" Hell, I'm not using anything new until I _wear out_ what I already have. Boycotts, marches, demonstrations, legal action, lobbying activities, voter registration, economic power: These are the traditional tools we've used to come this far, and we will continue to use them to achieve our objectives.

THOMAS: There is a move to eliminate black colleges and universities under the banner of integration. What is the NAACP's position on the survival of the black colleges?

HOOKS: The NAACP believes in integration of education from pre-kindergarten to post-Ph.D. But we have never and will never advocate the destruction of black colleges simply because at one point they were all black. We believe in strengthening and revitalizing these institutions. There are some supportive elements that historically and predominantly black colleges can give to certain students that the students may not get other places. Obviously, we think these schools ought to exist as integrated institutions, admitting whites as well as blacks. The NAACP is fighting now with the federal government, state governments, and private sources to make sure our schools are strengthened and enriched, so that they can attract students from everywhere.

Benjamin Hooks, Exec. Director of the NAACP leads a march to the South Carolina State House for ceremonies observing the 25th Anniversary of the U.S. Supreme Court's desegregation decision. *(Wide World Photos)*

THOMAS: The NAACP has also made a stand on energy. How does the energy crisis affect poor, elderly black people, and what is the NAACP doing about it?

HOOKS: When fuel is going sky-high and when people in big cities have to depend on natural gas or oil for heating, they often have to choose between eating enough or keeping warm. The NAACP, in February, 1977, was the first major black organization to suggest we ought to have an energy policy that would not forget the poor and the powerless in this nation. We were assailed by the leading journals of American thought: What in the world is the NAACP doing dealing with energy? That's not civil rights! But they now understand that if there is no energy and we have a fuelless economy, jobs will be lost, cities will be cold, and people will suffer.

The NAACP came up with a program called energy

stamps, similar to food stamps, which was accepted by the Carter administration. Stuart Eizenstat announced that without the NAACP's support, the measure never would have passed. That was a temporary measure. We are working with the administration now trying to get a more permanent program of fuel stamps so that those who are least able to afford the cost of energy will get some relief from the escalating price.

THOMAS: Frantz Fanon said any group oppressed to a large enough extent will rise against its oppressor. With unemployment, inflation, and social conditions being what they presently are in poor communities, is another hot summer of rioting and violence a possibility?

HOOKS: Yes, but first let me deal with your quotation. We quote a lot of people and anybody can say anything, but that doesn't make them an authority on it. I have read and studied Frantz Fanon. There are a lot of ways an oppressed people can rise, and a hot summer is not the only way to rise. One way to rise is to study, to be smarter than your oppressor. Another way is to get richer than your oppressor. If you read the history of the survival of the Jewish people, for thousands of years, until 1948, there was not a place in this whole world where Jews were not expendable. But they did not succumb to the philosophy that they had to use physical force as their only means of survival. The concept of rising against oppression through physical contact is stupid and self-defeating. It exalts brawn over brain. It exalts a man or woman's body over the mind. And the most enduring contributions made to civilization have not been made by brawn, they have been made by brain.

You look at the pyramids, and you think about how much physical strength it took to pile those blocks up. But before that could be done, somebody had to plan *how* it was going to be done. Before you can use physical strength you have to use your brain. Elephants are larger than humans, lions are stronger, polar bears are more vicious, and yet we control them, not by our brawn, but by our brain. The worst concept in the world is that rising against oppression means a physical uprising. I don't subscribe to that theory at all. I think there are many ways to rise against your oppressor.

I saw a movie once called *Sounder* that took place in the state of Louisiana in the mid-thirties. I saw this beautiful black woman, played by Cicely Tyson, rise to tremendous heights of superiority, and yet she never picked up a stick and hit a white man, or slapped a white woman. I believe in the superiority of the mind over brawn.

The rise against the oppressor may mean a short walk to the ballot box. It may mean that we can no longer afford the luxury of having 50 percent of the blacks in New York City not bothering to register to vote, and another 50 percent of those who have registered not bothering to vote, and then talking about a long, hot summer of violence. You know, long, hot summers don't produce as much in the long run as getting people into the legislature and the city council who can enact laws. I lived in Detroit and I lived in New York City, and they're light years apart in what they're doing, because in Detroit we've got a black mayor.

THOMAS: How do you communicate to young people that there's a great similarity between the rate of unemployment and the number of blacks who aren't registered to vote?

HOOKS: I suspect this is one of our most difficult problems. You used a great word: communication. I don't think we've been doing much communicating. We've been talking. Talking is not communicating; communication is a two-way street. It's a dialogue. It means if I talk, you listen and ask me something, and I listen to you and ask you something.

I lived in the state of Tennessee on the border of Mississippi in 1949, when black folks had practically no rights. I go back to Mississippi now and see seventeen blacks sitting in the legislature. I see Jim Eastland—he was the patriarch of the world, the great senator from

Mississippi—who didn't even run again because he knew that blacks could defeat him. I see the change that has been brought about in Mississippi because blacks used the weapons they had to bring about that change. And when they brought about that change it produced economic opportunity, it produced all kinds of things. When we talk about a long, hot summer, it seems to me that's a senseless and mindless way to try to deal with oppression.

Now, the fact of the matter is that the way things are going, we may have a long, hot summer. There may be violence in the streets. Certainly I don't want to see it, but I can understand people who feel powerless, deprived, helpless, dehumanized, and brutalized, their manhood or womanhood made a mockery of—I can understand how that wells up. There have been many times in my life where I've been so mistreated that I felt the only remedy was throwing a brick. I remember when I was an assistant public defender, and they were going to appoint a chief public defender in my court. They wouldn't give the job to me because I was black. They picked a young white lawyer who had just finished law school, who had never tried a case, and told him that he would be my boss. And I'd been practicing law for fifteen years! I never will forget that. I really wanted to take some dynamite and blow the courthouse down. But something else said, "If you use your head, you can beat this."

One year later, in that same courtroom where I couldn't be the head public defender, I was the judge, and the public defender had to come to me and say, "If your honor please." I had on the black robe and had the gavel in my hand. So there are better ways than throwing bricks to achieve what we want.

THOMAS: Mr. Hooks, with the presidential election approaching, a national conference for a black agenda for the 1980s was held in Richmond, Virginia, this past March. The sponsors invited each candidate for the Democratic and Republican presidential nominations to speak on the final day of the conference. Not one presidential candidate chose to show. Why was that?

HOOKS: I think the Republican party has decided that blacks are going to vote for Democrats no matter who they are. If a donkey ran for president on the Democratic ticket, the Republicans would come to the conclusion we'd vote for him—we've acted like it. Ninety-five percent of the black voters are going to vote for a Democratic candidate for president, no matter who it is. And so the Republican candidates don't see any advantage to be gained in seeking votes where there are none. The Democratic candidates assume they have the vote anyway. They take the black vote for granted.

If I were selling ice cream and I knew you had a rule in your house where under no condition could you buy ice cream—your wife couldn't buy any, and your children couldn't buy any—I'd waste a lot of time at your house trying to sell ice cream. On the other hand, if there were another house down the street where they'd come to me to buy ice cream, I wouldn't need to go to that house either. And that's the position we're in. The Republican party says, "You're not going to buy my ice cream so I'm not coming," the Democratic party says, "I can have my stand across town and you're going to hitchhike over there to buy my ice cream, so I won't waste my time coming to your house."

Down the road we'll have to figure out a way to prevent candidates from ignoring us. One of the ways is to present ourselves as six or seven million intelligent, particular, registered voters who will go to the polls in large numbers and vote for the candidate, regardless of party label, who will do that which is most essential to our progress and welfare.

We've got to become a political commodity that is independent, assertive and strong, voting our own self-interests as other ethnic groups do, and putting the nation on notice at the city, state, and national level: If you don't scratch our back, we won't scratch yours.

THOMAS: What is the NAACP doing in the area of voter registration and education?

HOOKS: Voter education and registration have been two of our strongest efforts. Across the past twenty years no organization has been more effective at voter registration than the NAACP. Joe Madison, a brilliant man, heads our voter education campaign and projects. One of the things we've tried to do is zero in on getting the state legislatures to make every high school principal a deputy registrar. That way, eighteen-year-olds who want to register won't have to go downtown, but can register right in school. We will have citizenship days to encourage them to do that.

Voter registration depends upon local chapters and local people. There's nothing easy about it. There has to be an organization, phone banks, knocking on doors, and car pools made available. Black colleges and universities could be a big help in our voter registration drives. If we could get the people power of all those students out there knocking on doors and calling people on the phone, I think we could make the whole world look and wonder at what's being done in voter registration.

THOMAS: Is reverse discrimination possible in regard to black people in the United States of America?

HOOKS: I maintain that the term "reverse discrimination" is one of the biggest lies ever perpetrated on the American public. Look at how far out of the mainstream blacks are in any given area. We are 2 percent of the doctors, 2 percent of the lawyers, one percent of the certified public accountants. In the 2,200 predominantly white universities there are fewer than 10 black presidents. Of the 1,700 daily newspapers, 80 percent don't have a black in any important capacity. Of the 7,000 commercial radio stations, only 70 are owned by blacks. Out of 700 commercial television stations, in the whole history of the FCC only one license has ever been granted to a black group. And I speak from firsthand knowledge.

With that kind of a background, how in the name of God are you going to have reverse discrimination? We've only just begun, and until we move a long way farther down the road, it's going to be impossible to talk about reverse discrimination.

THOMAS: We were talking earlier about integration. W.E.B. DuBois recognized the advantages of integration, but at the same time he warned blacks to protect and preserve their Africanness. Do you agree with that? Does that still hold true today?

HOOKS: I am a firm believer that we have to possess and we have to continue to nurture those traits that you call Africanness and that I call blackness—the traits that have distinguished us.

There used to be an expression that America was a great melting pot. The whole concept of the melting pot was that everything got thrown in there and melted down until you couldn't tell the difference between the original ingredients. We went along with that concept until it dawned on us one day that we were black, and no matter how you spell it, when you melt black with anything, everything ends up black. Black is strong. It predominates. One drop of black ink in a glass of water turns the whole glass a different color. And one drop of white water in a bottle of black ink doesn't do anything. Right? I mean, black is a strong thing. And it dawned on us in the mid-sixties that America wasn't going to let us melt into their melting pot, because all America would end up black.

So instead of being part of the melting pot, we started talking about being part of a tossed salad. You understand? There are carrots in a tossed salad, and bell peppers, cucumbers, lettuce, and tomatoes. Everything is tossed up together but nothing loses its own characteristics. If I have a good tossed salad, I want to be able to appreciate every bit of it for color, for beauty, for taste, and for health, but I don't want any part of it to lose its distinctive characteristics. Each racial group and each sex ought to be individual but still be a part of the whole. Because we started feeling that way, other ethnic groups—the Italians, the Polish, the Irish—are now all proud of their ethnic background.

I believe not in the melting pot concept, but rather in the tossed salad concept of integration. I'm an American, but I'm proud of my heritage and of those qualities which are uniquely African about me. I'm not ashamed that the blood of black people is my predominant characteristic. I agree with DuBois that we ought never to forget our unique character.

THOMAS: You're a great, dynamic, on-the-case brother. Keep on preaching, keep on teaching, keep on fighting, keep on telling it Like It Is.

May 13, 1980

NIKKI GIOVANNI

NIKKI GIOVANNI

> . . . I really hope no white person ever has cause
> to write about me
> because they never understand
> Black love is Black wealth and they'll
> probably talk about my hard childhood
> and never understand that
> all the while I was quite happy
>
> —from "Nikki-Rosa"

Nikki Giovanni—poet, author, recording artist, and lecturer—was born in Knoxville, Tennessee, and moved with her family to Cincinnati, Ohio, when she was two months old. She returned to Tennessee to spend time with her grandparents and, later, to attend Fisk University.

In her book *Gemini* she describes Knoxville:

When we were growing up, Knoxville didn't have television, let alone an airport. It finally got TV but the airport is in Alcoa. And is now called Tyson Field. Right? Small towns are funny. Knoxville even has a zip code and seven-digit phone numbers. All of which seems strange to me since I mostly remember Mrs. Flora Ford's white cake with white icing and Miss Delaney's blue furs and Armetine Picket's being the sharpest woman in town—she attended our church—and Miss Brooks wearing tight sweaters and Carter-Roberts Drug Store sending out Modern Jazz Quartet sounds of "Fontessa" and my introduction to Nina Simone by David Cherry, dropping a nickel in the jukebox and "Porgy" coming out.

At Fisk, Ms. Giovanni was a founding member of the university chapter of SNCC, the Student Non-Violent Coordinating Committee. In the following interview she says, "I'm of the generation that was considered crazy." But out of the turbulent sixties, Ms. Giovanni emerged as a major poetic spokesperson for blacks in America. Her poetry is variously violent, bitter, joyful, and melancholy. Her writing deals with love between black men and women and between all black people, the black liberation movement, rhythm and blues music, her childhood and her family. Weaving in and out of these themes is a central focus on individualism. Who am I? What am I? Her work has been called a search for individual values in the black community.

In addition to ten books of poems, Ms. Giovanni has published *Gemini*, a book of autobiographical essays, and two books of conversations: *A Dialogue, James Baldwin and Nikki Giovanni* and *A Poetic Equation: Conversations Between Nikki Giovanni and Margaret Walker*. One of her four record albums, *Truth Is on Its Way*, won the N.A.T.R.A. award for the best spoken word album in 1972. Ms. Giovanni holds honorary doctorates from several colleges and universities. She received the *Mademoiselle* magazine award for outstanding achievement, and was honored for youth leadership as Woman of the Year by *Ladies Home Journal* magazine in 1972. Her book of poems, *My House*, has been commended by the American Library Association as one of the best books for young adults.

In addition to writing and recording, Ms. Giovanni has taught creative writing at Livingston College of Rutgers University. She is an editorial consultant for *Encore American and Worldwide News*, and is also a syndicated columnist for the Anderson-Moberg Syndicate of *The New York Times*.

INTERVIEW
NIKKI GIOVANNI

ARTHUR THOMAS: Nikki, many forces are determined to wipe out black colleges, to wipe out black people, to wipe out poor and oppressed people—these are very bad times. Which poems of yours best describes what's happening now?

NIKKI GIOVANNI: I haven't written a poem. I think these are prosaic times in terms of the situation you describe, but I am not the right person for you to talk to. I'm really not on the downhill side of any of it. I'm very optimistic. Whenever it bottoms out we can do nothing but go up.

It's probably fair to say that Jimmy Carter has been an insensitive president and this has been a slow and stupid Congress, to put it mildly. But we as a people have made certain decisions that I certainly do applaud. I could not help but applaud Miami.* We simply have to make a statement that the killing of black people is not right, that you cannot just run into somebody on the street and decide that four or five of you will jump him and stomp him. To protect the right of four cops, four policemen, to kill a black man, it cost them $100 million. Now they know the price. The next black man they kill, it's going to be another $100 million. Now you can say, "Well, I don't live in Dade County, I don't have to pay for that," but you have insurance. You pay taxes. You're going to pay for it. It's going to come back.

Now I would suggest, if the world were right, that what it is, is too expensive to kill a black person. Miami has sent

---

*The Miami riots in May, 1980, were sparked by the acquittal of four white ex-county officers charged with the beating death of black Miami businessman Arthur McDuffie. The riots took the lives of eighteen people, and caused over $100 million in damages.

us a message—all of us. And that message is: We don't want you to shoot our boys. You know what I'm saying?

I'm very optimistic about Miami. I would be sad if they had taken it, if they had turned those four white people loose and they'd come back into Dade County and they'd say, "Yeah, we're the cops, we're going to kill you." No, I'm very happy about Miami. It made my day.

I am optimistic because I am happy about the young people. I went to Fisk University. I'm happy about what I see at my institution. I'm happy about the United Negro College Fund, and their fund-raising this year.

We have to take care of ourselves. Nobody else is going to do it. I feel that we are now getting that message. I'm high on it. I'm excited.

THOMAS: What is your advice to black people? What can we do to improve our own existence here?

GIOVANNI: I am essentially a metaphysician. And I think that one of the things we have to do is reconceptualize who we are. We are simply overdue for a new idea of *what* it is to be alive. *Who* is alive? *What* is a human being? How does that differ from a plant, or from another mammal, or from anything else? How do we come together, we who are alive, with that which is alive? How do we justify our poisoning of the air with atomic substances? How do we justify that? How do we justify Three Mile Island, where thirty thousand gallons of radiated water leaked into the Ohio River?

THOMAS: We need to be responsible for our lives and our environment. What do you mean when you tell students to be responsible for themselves?

GIOVANNI: That the world is theirs. I'm saying that the world is yours. And I think that we in the black community have simply failed to remind black youngsters that the world is theirs.

I'm of the generation that was considered crazy, and

that was probably an understatement. When we came out in the sixties we said, "Hey, we are really tired of looking at those signs that say colored waiting room, colored drinking fountain, colored ticket counter, no colored allowed. There must be a better way." And ninety students in SNCC, the Student Non-Violent Coordinating Committee, said, "We're going to change it. We're going to do something about it." But before the ninety students in SNCC said it, four young men in Greensboro said, "I'm going to go and sit down and I'm going to have a cup of coffee."* Now it's very chic, these days, to laugh at the coffee war. But when you look at the students we produced in the seventies, they couldn't have done that. If it had been up to them to have broken down segregation in a Woolworth's or a Grant's or to have gone to the bus station in Nashville, Tennessee—it wouldn't have happened. We did it.

I'm saying we believe that the world is ours. It's your life—take it. Lead it to your fullest. I'm trying to lead it to my fullest.

THOMAS: Do students today utilize the gains that were made during the sixties?

GIOVANNI: We've had absolute slippage.

I'm optimistic about students today. The young people I see coming to school now are much more committed. But for the last ten or twelve years we've had students who, if they didn't eat it, sleep with it, or drive it, they didn't care about it. And I think that's a disgraceful statement.

I look at the number of cars on predominantly black campuses. I'm not against cars, I think they're a nice way to get around—inefficient but nice. I was on the board of

---

*On a February morning in 1960, a group of students from North Carolina A & T sat down at a white-only lunch counter in Greensboro, North Carolina, and refused to leave until they were served. Greensboro was the first direct student action to break color lines in the South, and inspired sit-ins in places ranging from bus stations and lunch counters to churches.

Hampton Institute, and when I saw that 65 percent of our students were on scholarships or some sort of financial aid, but 77 or 78 percent of our students had automobiles, I couldn't understand it. How can you justify an automobile when you're on aid? We're not here to provide for you that which we don't have. Now maybe if you went to Harvard, maybe if you had money, it might be different. But we don't. We have produced a whole generation, a decade of people who think the world owes them something. I'm not going to say the world doesn't. I'm just going to say you can't collect it.

THOMAS: I visit elementary and high schools quite a bit, and when I talk to youngsters about Martin Luther King, Jr., or about Malcolm X, about Stokely Carmichael, H. Rap Brown, or Fred Hampton, they say, "We don't want to hear about that; that happened during the old times. What's that got to do with me?" How do we turn that around?

GIOVANNI: That's a problem I think we are not going to continue to face. Young people are saying, "I really do want to know who I am." There is a reason why "Roots I" and "Roots II" were the number one and number two most watched shows on television. There is a reason. I think it's because people are saying, "I am interested now."

The question for the writer, which is my profession, is how do we present a Fred Hampton and a Mark Clark? How do we present an H. Rap Brown? How do we present a Martin Luther King? Because we were not very pleased with how other people presented King. We as writers and we as producers have to say, "These are our heroes and this is how we produce them. This is how we handle it."

THOMAS: It seems that white people can very easily be defined as black man's burden today.

GIOVANNI: Oh, yes, I would agree.

Poet Nikki Giovanni

THOMAS: If five of the most powerful white world leaders came to you and said, "Miss Giovanni, we recognize that we are in trouble, we know that everything is going wrong. Please give us some advice in terms of turning things around, because our survival is at stake, too," what would your advice to them be?

GIOVANNI: I'm not in the position of advising people who have historically been my oppressors. I'm just not going to do it. It's not what I do in life.

Now, if you're asking me what advice I'm going to give students, I'm going to say: Think. I'm going to say that you are inherently a worthwhile human being. You don't have to prove that.

While I was in philosophy in college there was a

question, and I used to drive my teacher crazy: You're on a big ship and the ship is sinking. There is a lifeboat that can only hold eight people. There are nine of you. What would you do?

All of my classmates would immediately begin to say, "So and so would have to go," or those who were calling themselves brave would say, "I would jump overboard and die." I said, "There must be a solution. If there are nine of us with a lifeboat that only holds eight, there must be a solution." And the professor would say, because I made a C in that course, "That is not an answer." I said, "When I get to the point that I am on a big ship and there are nine of us with a lifeboat that holds eight, then I would deal with that. But I will not sit here and kill somebody for the convenience of this class."

You cannot accept somebody else's premises on what your life could be.

THOMAS: Nikki, according to sociologist Robert Staples, there are approximately 732,000 more black women than black men right now between the ages of twenty-four and forty-four. Brothers are victimized by suicide, by homicide, and by being thrown into jail, many times unjustly. In a certain category there's one black male to every five females. Does that, in your opinion, create a problem for our community?

GIOVANNI: When we deal with black men and black women, the first thing that gets brought up is statistics. The male of the species is always in short supply. That is not unusual to black people, it is not unusual to America, it's not unusual to anything. The male is basically an aggressive animal, and nature balances on a number of things.

When we start to talk about human beings, and we're talking at this point about black human beings, statistics are not what we are talking about. Because black women do not belong to black men.

If I had a daughter, my primary responsibility to her would be to remind her that she belongs to herself and that she is not obligated to search only among the black American community for a love object. I can't even think like that. First of all, if she just wants somebody black, there are lots of other black people. But there are lots of other people as well, and love being such a precious commodity, if she would find love, I would be happy for her.

If I thought black women belonged to black men, I would have to be upset when I saw a black man with a white woman. You remember people seeing black men with white women and saying, "We're not going to let our men . . ." I say, hey, these men don't belong to us. They belong to themselves.

We need to stop thinking in terms of possessiveness, with men thinking, "That's my woman," and women thinking, "Those are my men." You can't have a relationship with people who think about you that way. What's the difference between that and, "That's my slave"? Or, "Those are my peasants"? It's crazy. We reject it when white people say, "Those are my niggers," but we will take that same thought and say, "You are my woman." It doesn't make sense.

THOMAS: Nikki, would you read us a few of your poems?

GIOVANNI: Okay. I'll read "EGO TRIPPING (there may be a reason why)."

> I was born in the congo
> I walked to the fertile crescent and built
>   the sphinx
> I designed a pyramid so tough that a star
>   that only glows every one hundred years falls
>   into the center giving divine perfect light
> I am bad
>
> I sat on the throne
>   drinking nectar with allah

I got hot and sent an ice age to europe
     to cool my thirst
My oldest daughter is nefertiti
     the tears from my birth pains
     created the nile
I am a beautiful woman

I gazed on the forest and burned
     out the sahara desert
     with a packet of goat's meat
     and a change of clothes
I crossed it in two hours
I am a gazelle so swift
     so swift you can't catch me

     For a birthday present when he was three
I gave my son hannibal an elephant
     He gave me rome for mother's day
My strength flows ever on

My son noah built new/ark and
I stood proudly at the helm
     as we sailed on a soft summer day
I turned myself into myself and was
     jesus
     men intone my loving name
     All praises All praises
I am the one who would save

I sowed diamonds in my back yard
My bowels deliver uranium
     the filings from my fingernails are
     semi-precious jewels
     On a trip north
I caught a cold and blew

My nose giving oil to the arab world
I am so hip even my errors are correct
I sailed west to reach east and had to round off
    the earth as I went
      The hair from my head thinned and gold was laid
      across three continents

I am so perfect so divine so ethereal so surreal
I cannot be comprehended
    except by my permission

I mean . . . I . . . can fly
    like a bird in the sky . . .

GIOVANNI: This next poem is called "My House."

i only want to
be there to kiss you
as you want to be kissed
when you need to be kissed
where i want to kiss you
cause it's my house
and i plan to live in it

i really need to hug you
when i want to hug you
as you like to hug me
does this sound like a silly poem

i mean it's my house
and i want to fry pork chops
and bake sweet potatoes
and call them yams
cause i run the kitchen
and i can stand the heat

i spent all winter in
carpet stores gathering

patches so i could make
a quilt
does this really sound
like a silly poem

i mean i want to keep you
warm

and my windows might be dirty
but it's my house
and if i can't see out sometimes
they can't see in either

english isn't a good language
to express emotion through
mostly i imagine because people
try to speak english instead
of trying to speak through it
i don't know maybe it is
a silly poem

i'm saying it's my house
and i'll make fudge and call
it love and touch my lips
to the chocolate warmth
and smile at old men and call
it revolution cause what's real
is really real
and i still like men in tight
pants cause everybody has some
thing to give and more
important need something to take

and this is my house and you make me
happy
so this is your poem

THOMAS: You are a student of space. Where are we going in that direction?

GIOVANNI: We're not going to fly off into space until we can live on earth. We're not going to live here on earth until we understand there is more to earth than the human species. Mankind in his great arrogance has assumed that life is only about him. That's too limited. Black people have said, and if you read the literature you'll see that black people have said, "I don't want to be limited to black people." White people have said, "I don't want to be limited to white people." So they all feel very liberal when they get involved with some other race. But that's just another person. I mean, what's the difference?

The human species is not the only living thing on this earth. The flora and the fauna are not the only living things. We're talking about elements that are alive. What right do we have to pollute an ocean and cause something else to die? Evolution is about the species adapting to earth, not to man.

But mankind has a great arrogance. And we have problems because we have always delineated life as particular to our group.

In the black community it gets to be real crazy, because they deal with life on their block. If it's not about their block, they don't know it. Remember the old days with the black gangs and a black kid from another block would come in and could get killed? Now this is crazy! That doesn't make sense. White folks do the same thing.

Something is wrong here. I'm not putting anybody in a bind. I'm not taking anybody on. I'm just saying that we who are alive have to be about living.

THOMAS: In articles on the future, futurists do not say anything about blacks. The implication is that blacks will not be a part of the future. When you ask futurists questions about racism, they say it is not important. How are we going to fit into the future?

GIOVANNI: We have to decide where we want to be.

What excites me about the black community is that we are an emotional people, that we do an awful lot from the heart. Sometimes that's helpful, sometimes it's not, but if I had to choose between the black community and any other I would choose the black American community, because we will go for the gut feeling. We will say, "Yes, this is right." If a colony of Martians was going to come to earth I would recommend they land in Lincoln Heights, Ohio, because it's a black community and if they go and live and don't bother anybody people will eventually say, "Hey, man, I've got some tomato plants. You need some?" We're not hard to get along with. Whereas if they moved in a white community, somebody would make a zoning ordinance: We don't want any aliens.

There is strength in the black community. What excites me about the new crop of black presidents we have at our black institutions is that they are once again saying, "We must teach leadership." And when we start to talk about leadership, we're not talking about, vote for me and I'll set you free. We're talking about the idea that this community has strength. And we must begin to understand what those strengths are.

Howell Raines* took his tape recorder and went down to Mississippi to write his book on the South. He was going to talk to old black men and say, what was it like to be a man in Mississippi? Now, he didn't want to know what it was like to be a _man_ in Mississippi, he wanted to know, what was it like when everything says that you aren't a man to assume that somehow you are. In other words, _How did you live?_ Not, what did you eat. How did you live? You understand what I'm saying?

We have lived under horrendous circumstances. We

---

*Southern journalist and author of _My Soul Is Rested: Movement Days in the Deep South Remembered_ (New York: Putnam, 1977), an oral history of the civil rights movement in the South.

cannot now give up that strength, that spiritualism, that idea of pulling together. We cannot give that up just because we've moved into cities. We have to hold on to that which we had in Mississippi, Georgia, and Alabama—a sense of family, not in the sense of "You're my brother and I'm your sister, we came out of the same mother and father," but in the sense of "We are together." And I submit, because I am a southerner, that we did not base our love of each other on any fear of white people, but on our caring about each other. They've tried to turn that around on us for the last twenty years, saying that the only reason the black community came together is that they were scared of white folks. Well, if that were the case, we would still be together. Because they're still getting crazy! There was obviously something else. We cared about each other. We would take the chance.

When I grew up in Knoxville, Tennessee, if I didn't go to school on time the right way, before I made the first wrong turn my grandmother had a phone call, "Your grand-daughter just went down my street." People didn't mind taking the chance.

THOMAS: We've got to move back to that.

GIOVANNI: Of course we do. We've got to move, not back into it, but *forward* into it, because the city experience is going to be different from a rural experience.

THOMAS: Nikki, you are a beautiful lady. Keep on forcing us to think, keep on communicating, keep on agitating, keep on telling it "Like It Is."

June 3, 1980

ALVIN POUSSAINT

BIOGRAPHY
ALVIN POUSSAINT

Dr. Alvin Poussaint, a professor of psychiatry and associate dean of student affairs at Harvard Medical School, uses psychiatry to understand the black personality and racism in America. The black American, he says, is torn in two directions: "an American, a Negro; two souls, two thoughts; two unreconciled strivings; two warring ideals in one dark body, whose dogged strength alone keeps it from being torn asunder."*

Alvin Poussaint became an avid reader at an early age. He excelled in mathematics and science in junior high school, and he was accepted at New York's prestigious Stuyvesant High School, where he realized the difference between the world of school and the world of his community. At Columbia University he encountered social exclusion because of his color. In medical school, as the only black in a class of eighty-six students, he saw the social exclusion deepen into more obvious racism. Poussaint found himself faced with professors who doubted his ability, as a black, to handle his work. He committed himself to a study of racism through psychiatry.

Poussaint served his internship at the Neuropsychiatric Institute of the University of California at Los Angeles. In his last year he was selected chief resident, and became the head of the institute's intern training program.

In the early sixties, Dr. Poussaint joined the members of the Student Non-Violent Coordinating Committee (SNCC) in working for civil rights in the South. There, Dr. Poussaint "saw black powerlessness in the face of white power. He saw liberal whites assuming—falsely—that they were to lead a black movement. He saw the price that had to be paid for a few

---

*Dr. Alvin Poussaint, quoted in the Ebony Success Library, Volume II: Famous Blacks Give Secrets of Success, by the editors of Ebony (Chicago: Johnson Publishing Company, Inc., 1973), p. 205.

moments of assertive black manhood and realized the psycho-sexual dimensions of the racial problem between blacks and whites. And wondered, 'What are we to do with our rage?' "*

Dr. Poussaint's numerous academic publications and popular articles focus on subjects including black suicide, education and black self-image, anger, and how whites can help end racism. Dr. Poussaint serves as health consultant to the Congressional Black Caucus, and as a member of the board of trustees of Operation PUSH (People United to Serve Humanity). He is on the editorial boards of several journals, and has written two books: *Why Blacks Kill Blacks*, in 1972, and *Black Child Care*, with J. P. Comer in 1975.

---

*Ibid., p. 204.

INTERVIEW
DR. ALVIN POUSSAINT

ARTHUR THOMAS: Dr. Poussaint, black males are catching it from everywhere. Is there a deliberate attempt to wipe out black males?

ALVIN POUSSAINT: Black males have been the focus of a lot of the oppression back from slavery. Oppression always works primarily from the men to the men. The men have to be controlled because they are potentially the soldiers who will fight back.

The oppression toward black men is special. It is showing up in many ways that black men are in a lot of trouble. They have a rising suicide rate. They are the ones who are primarily unemployed. They are the ones with the social ills that have to do with drug addiction and alcoholism. They are easily arrested by the police and sent to jail. They have a rising homicide rate.

THOMAS: That sounds like something that occurred in the forties, fifties, and sixties. Do these conditions still exist today?

POUSSAINT: They exist today. Some of them, as a matter of fact, are getting worse. The suicide rate is going up and so is the homicide rate, accounting for the leading cause of death among young black males. So it is a serious problem. Also, the life expectancy of black men overall is about sixty-one or sixty-two years old, which is on the low side.

THOMAS: So a black man is not going to live to retirement because he is going to die when he is about sixty years old?

POUSSAINT: Actually, there are a lot of black men, of course, who live into their seventies. But the overall life expectancy rate is brought down because there are so many black men who are dying when they are young. When you average it together, the life expectancy is very low.

THOMAS: Some civil rights activists and civil rights leaders don't see the Bakke decision as being a very serious one, as far as negative consequences for the black community are concerned. How do you feel about the Bakke decision?

POUSSAINT: The Bakke decision has had serious impact, negative impact, on affirmative action programs in professional schools and in colleges. A number of minority admissions programs have been dismantled since the Bakke decision. Although we don't know yet what's going to happen next year, it would appear that because the programs have been changed and restructured, minority admissions and black admissions will probably go down in those institutions. Minority admissions are already on the downswing through medical schools this year.

THOMAS: What can black professionals and the black community do to deal with lowering minority admissions to medical schools?

POUSSAINT: They have to do something similar to what the NAACP plans to do, and that is to monitor all affirmative action programs in their community to make sure the Bakke decision isn't used as an excuse for backsliding.

THOMAS: Why are white people so opposed to there being more black doctors when there is only one black doctor in this country for every five thousand black people? Do they simply want us to die from lack of proper health care?

POUSSAINT: I don't think that's the issue they think they're dealing with. I think they mainly see it in a competitive way. There's a limited number of seats in professional schools, and they want those seats, and they will compete against anybody for them.

THOMAS: But doesn't that translate out to mean the fewer black doctors we have, the more black people who will die?

POUSSAINT: It could. In a lot of urban centers and rural areas, it has been black doctors who have provided health care for black people.

THOMAS: So an attitude designed to make sure there are not enough seats in medical schools for black people is in fact an attitude designed to ensure that black people keep dying seven years earlier than white people.

POUSSAINT: That's some of the effect of it. If black people don't get good health care—and they get it from both whites and blacks, but it is a fact that black doctors have worked with the black community—then you're going to see some ill effects. It's still a problem in urban centers everywhere that blacks don't get good health care, they don't get good emergency care, and that leads to deaths. It is not just a black problem. It has to do with how the health care system is organized.

THOMAS: Why is the black suicide rate increasing?

POUSSAINT: We don't know the exact answer to that. It is partly because low-income black males, and black males in general, have rising expectations. They thought the civil rights movement was going to bring a lot. But instead there is much more black unemployment and disintegration of the black community. So we have a deterioration of the whole community atmosphere, and however you name it, the lack of jobs tends to boost up the suicide rate.

It's interesting that the suicide rate is mostly going up in young black males from nineteen to twenty-four, and not in the older group of black males. It seems that many young males have to make it as adults or make it in the society, and many of them say "To heck with it all," and they kill themselves. Frequently the suicides occur after some type of confrontation with authority, that is, getting jailed or arrested, something that makes them feel hopeless and in great despair.

THOMAS: What is the reason for the rise in black-on-black crime? Why are we hurting each other? Why are we robbing each other? Why are we killing each other?

POUSSAINT: Partly for the same reasons which are causing a rising suicide rate, but there's also a direct relationship between the rising homicide rate and the increased availability of handguns. Years ago we had few murders from handguns. Now handguns are all around. And when you pull the trigger there's no retracting your anger. That's one of the reasons.

I think we still have a problem with not feeling good about ourselves. When you face increased unemployment, you get more idle youths and people standing around angry and frustrated.

THOMAS: Your research has shown that in some cases it is just as important for youngsters to believe they can control their fate as it is for them to have a positive self-attitude or image.

POUSSAINT: That's true. Though self-concept is important, I think we have put too much emphasis on positive self-concepts in people without looking at the other ingredients that make for success or achievement or survival. And one of the things apparently that makes for survival is to have a sense that you can control your environment, that you can assert yourself in that environment and accomplish something, that you don't take the attitude of a victim, but of someone who can overcome.

THOMAS: Can we relate black-on-black crime in America to what is happening in other parts of the world? In Africa, the predominantly black Rhodesian army is shooting and killing the black guerillas who are fighting for liberation from the white regime. Why are black men fighting against each other?

POUSSAINT: I think it demonstrates the power of conditioning an oppressive regime can put on black folks. I think, frankly, a lot of the soldiers are involved for mercenary reasons, that is, to make some money, and this is held over their heads by the white regime. "Here, this is a way for you to make some money and get a little power in the system." They are holding out to them some chance of shared power, even though the whites will remain in control.

Sometimes we are too ready to turn on each other. We've had similar experiences in the United States, where blacks will turn on other blacks. Blacks will infiltrate the civil rights movement and then try to destroy it under the direction of the FBI. It is an international issue that has to do with the nature of our psyche, and also the forces controlling it.

THOMAS: FBI infiltration of the black liberation movement seems to relate to a sense of powerlessness.

POUSSAINT: It adds to a sense of powerlessness and also adds to the sense of paranoia, which in itself can be disruptive to organizing or getting things done. It makes us realize that there are certain institutional forces with a lot of power that can effectively disrupt and destroy. It's a bitter pill to swallow, but is part of the reality for black people and other groups in the country who challenge the government or the system in a fashion that is threatening to it. You can expect that the FBI and the CIA will protect what they feel are their interests.

America is not necessarily more liberal than the countries we label oppressive. America has a history of oppressing left-wing people. A communist here is dealt with very severely. You will not find many people willing to admit they are communists—they would be labeled, spied on, watched. The message in this is that we aren't allowed to think about all of our options, to think freely and discuss things, because we narrow our vision based on what the government says we can and cannot do.

Dr. Alvin Poussaint, psychiatrist and associate dean of Student Affairs at Harvard Medical School.

THOMAS: Do black students on predominantly white campuses have special problems?

POUSSAINT: They have to deal with special psychological pressures. They probably have to think more about self-doubt. They have to worry whether the administrators really want them there, or whether they are there only because of affirmative action. They also have to deal with psychological insults and assaults that have to do with the sometimes negative attitudes of professors and sometimes negative attitudes of white students.

They feel in the minority, and sometimes feel socially uncomfortable. They have to decide how they're going to lead their social lives, including things like socializing with whites. They may also be in a system where they feel the reward comes by imitating the white styles as much as possible, and that can be a pressure as well.

THOMAS: Are black males and black females victimized by similar problems?

POUSSAINT: Black females and black males are victimized a bit differently. Right now one of the big problems on campus is that there are many more black females than there are black males. On some campuses black females outnumber the males five to one, seven to one. This creates a problem not only socially, but also influences how the black female may view the black male and how he views himself. He may have more self-doubts. It may draw them into a battle of the sexes and into competition with each other. Also, the issue of interracial dating comes up all the time.

THOMAS: What is the present state of the black family?

POUSSAINT: The black family, in my opinion, is in difficulty. I think the main difficulty right now is economic, even when two parents are working. Single-parent families especially face economic difficulties. The number of single-parent families has risen. I'm not saying these families can't bring up good children, but they are usually under economic hardship. The mother is under stress and overwhelmed from the responsibilities because she's the only breadearner, or she's on some type of government assistance and she doesn't have enough support.

And then we are in trouble because we have more children born out of wedlock. Fifty percent of black babies were born out of wedlock last year, which means very young black women, fourteen, fifteen, sixteen years old are having children, and they are just children themselves trying to raise them. I call it the "doll syndrome," because I think they see it as solving some of their problems, their need for attention and love, and for someone to care for themselves.

THOMAS: Why can't a country that can rebuild Germany, that can find a way to go to the moon, that can sell anything it wants to sell, develop a strategy to communicate to young people the importance of not having babies when they are too young? The importance of respecting oneself and others? What is the reason that we can attack those problems that we choose to attack so successfully, but we ignore the poor and the oppressed?

POUSSAINT: It is part of the tradition in this country that you do ignore the poor, and you ignore minorities who are oppressed. In fact, it is part of the tradition to say that they are responsible for their own condition, and not to pay enough attention to the social forces that produce the conditions. I agree with you that programs to deal with many of these problems have been woefully inadequate, and demonstrate a lack of commitment on the part of the government, both federal government, local governments, and even the private sector, to cope with these problems. It's part of an individualistic attitude in this country. People are selfish and think about themselves. They say, "If you are comfortable and doing well, then forget about the people who haven't made it."

THOMAS: How can economically successful blacks help less successful blacks?

POUSSAINT: What successful blacks can do the most is to be politically active in their communities and nationally, because the problem of black unemployment is mainly due to lack of opportunity and the lack of availability of employment. Those are institutional things that have to be changed.

   We have to think more creatively. We can't just accept the answer that the government puts out: "There has to be this rate of unemployment because otherwise there will be inflation."

The other thing successful blacks can do insofar as they are involved in businesses, corporations, and other activities, is actively push to make their organizations have programs to hire, to train, and to include blacks. I don't think enough pressure is being applied in the private sector, or even the public sector, to force them to do more hiring.

There is still a wish to push blacks out. I don't think it's only a question of blacks not having the skills. That's an overall rationale. There are many, many whites without skills who have jobs and are absorbed into the system because they have people watching out for them. The notion of qualifications has been heavily laid on blacks. In the past they didn't talk about it too much, because the system frequently operates through patronage, and still does. Both in political sectors and in private sectors, people help friends and give friends jobs.

THOMAS: We have been attacking our people for not voting. You say that psychologically you can understand why a lot of our people don't vote.

POUSSAINT: Yes, I can. Traditionally they haven't been in the voting system and they couldn't vote, so they haven't established voting traditions. Also, after voting in a lot of elections, they look around them and they don't see anything changed. Things don't get better. They may decide they don't really gain very much from voting at all, so they have no motivation to vote.

Poor people in Los Angeles didn't turn out to vote against Proposition 13 because they didn't really understand how it would affect them. This involves education. We still can do much more to get out the black vote.

THOMAS: Dr. Poussaint, thank you for your insight, and thank you for "Like It Is."

December 15, 1978

PARREN MITCHELL

BIOGRAPHY
PARREN MITCHELL

Parren J. Mitchell, Maryland's first black representative and the
second black representative from a southern or border state in
nearly one hundred years, bases his work in Congress on a
straightforward political philosophy. "Every black elected official must have a simple credo: I am elected from a mixed district,
part white, part black; I will serve all the people. But I will give
my priority to black people and the poor because they need
more." Making blacks his priority and working to improve their
economic and employment opportunities has earned the fifty-
eight-year-old bachelor the title of "Mr. Minority Enterprise."

Mitchell is used to fighting for what he believes in. In 1950,
at age twenty-seven, he sued the University of Maryland to
enroll him as its first black graduate student. After completing
his master's degree in sociology there, he returned to teach at his
alma mater, Morgan State University.

In the late 1960s, Mitchell became executive director of
Baltimore's antipoverty program. He also served as executive
secretary for the Maryland Human Relations Commission,
playing the pivotal role in the enactment and implementation of
Maryland's statewide Public Accommodations Law.

In 1970 Mitchell was elected representative from Maryland's seventh district, which comprises two-thirds of the city of
Baltimore. In that race Mitchell captured 37 percent of the
Jewish vote and 80 percent of the black vote in his district.
According to Mitchell, "It showed sophistication and maturity
by the white portion of the district in its willingness to accept the
full participation of Negroes in the political process. And it
showed that the black community is unified and is using the

same moves that every other minority has done to achieve political power."*

In his ten years in Congress, Mitchell has become best known for his unending work on behalf of minority enterprise and employment. He wants not merely to get blacks public sector jobs, but also to make blacks job-creators. In 1976 he attached to President Carter's $4 billion Public Works Bill an amendment that earmarked 10 percent of the funds for minority businesses. That single amendment resulted in more than $625 million (15 percent) going to minority contractors, subcontractors, and suppliers.

He also introduced the legislation for Public Law 95–507, which President Carter signed into law in 1978. Up to that time federal agencies had done less than one percent of their procurement from minority firms. Public Law 95–507 required proposals from contractors to spell out their goals for awarding contracts to minority subcontractors. The law potentially provides billions of dollars for minority businesses.

In the House of Representatives, Congressman Mitchell has been a member of the House Budget Committee, vice-chairman of the Joint Committee on Defense Production, and chairman of the Congressional Black Caucus. His present positions include Whip-at-Large; senior member of the House Banking, Finance, and Urban Affairs Committee; chairman of the Small Business Committee's task force on minority enterprise; and chairman of the Congressional Black Caucus Subcommittee on Housing, Minority Enterprise, and Economic Development. He is on the Presidential Commission on the National Agenda for the Eighties.

---

*Michael Anders, "No Bands, Frills—Just a Victory," *Washington Evening Star*, November, 1970. Quoted in the Ralph Nader Congress Project, *Citizens Look at Congress. Parren J. Mitchell: Democratic Representative from Maryland.* Written by Linda M. Kupferstein (Washington, D.C.: Grossman Publishers, 1972), Vol. IV.

PARREN MITCHELL

ARTHUR THOMAS: Congressman Mitchell, do you feel there is a deliberate attempt by this country to keep black people in their place, to keep them from sharing the power and opportunities this country has to offer? In other words, does this country have a strategy for containment?

PARREN MITCHELL: Look at black unemployment. No matter what the economy was, black unemployment has always been twice as high as the white rate for the last thirty-five years. Is that not containment and destruction? Of all the black elected officials in this country, at any level, we make up maybe one percent of the total of elected officials in this country. Is that not containment and destruction? Look at the black businesses in America. The smallest of the Fortune 500 companies, the big white firms, could buy up all of the black businesses in America and still have profit left over. Is that not containment and destruction? Of course it is.

Containment is a question of not wanting to share power. When blacks eat in a restaurant, it's all right. We are consuming, but we aren't sharing the power; we're paying money to someone to give them more power. When we watch TV, we're not sharing power. We are an audience paying TV.

THOMAS: The depiction of blacks on TV—grinning, telling jokes—is that part of what you believe to be containment?

MITCHELL: That's psychological containment.

I think a whole lot of black people fail to realize some basic social psychology. Why do you laugh at something? Somebody throws a pie in somebody's face, why do you laugh? You laugh because you say, "Look how dumb he is to let that happen to him." You view what you laugh at as inferior. And therefore when blacks are paraded out on these shows in a way that doesn't even resemble black life as I know it, TV is creating a mentality that says blacks are inferior and therefore they are a subject to be laughed at.

THOMAS: Are there any exceptions?

MITCHELL: There are a few. You can't just totally denigrate an entire race of people, so you throw out a little something. You throw out "Miss Jane Pittman," that's a good honest show. Or you throw out "Roots," that's a good honest show. But those are just specials. The ongoing shows are the ones that portray us as fools. I don't see black teenagers acting like JJ. My father didn't act like Sanford. No way. He was a dignified black man. But the stereotyped roles are the ones that are constantly portrayed for us.

What hurts me the most is when black folks laugh at those shows. We laugh at ourselves being portrayed as fools. That's almost as damaging as containment.

THOMAS: Some of the few success models we have also keep us where we are. A great deal of attention is being given to the black "middle class." Is that part of the containment scheme?

MITCHELL: Yes, in fact, that's a gimmick. Let me tell you the way it's done. If a doctor knows that something is really not wrong with somebody, the doctor gives them a placebo. It's sugar and water. The doctor says, "Take that and you'll be fine." The patient thinks he's taking medicine, and gets better.

In order to contain the black community we point out a number of middle-class accomplishments, just enough to make blacks say, "Maybe I'm wrong if I'm not making it. These others are making it." But the unfairness of the media is that it doesn't show blacks living in abject poverty. It doesn't show the frustrations that we deal with every day. It doesn't show how we are forced to live because of a planned recession in America. That's the unfairness.

THOMAS: There are some key words that are particularly applied to blacks. People talk about "welfare" for black people, but "guaranteed loans" for automotive industries. Is that another sign of containment?

MITCHELL: There are a lot of key words. Many of them started when Nixon was running for president. He started using words like "crime in the streets." He was going to stop that. And white middle-class America didn't even have to think; they said, "Oh, they're talking about black people." "Welfare cheats and chiselers." Those were the code words. And we continue to use code words, negative code words for blacks, and positive code words for whites who become welfare recipients. I'm talking about corporations that come and ask the government for handouts.

THOMAS: What has happened to the minds of some black people who say things like, "I don't want low-cost housing in my area," or, "I don't want some of those black kids to go to school with my black kids," or, "The main problem in America is economics, not racism." Are they agents of those who are trying to contain us?

MITCHELL: At least they are unwitting agents, if not knowing agents. I don't know what's happened to their minds, I just call them fools. Just plain fools. Remember the Bakke case? Everybody got all excited about reverse discrimination and people were scared to death about it. Brothers I hadn't seen in years who had become middle-management executives in big corporations, executives in government, would come by my office, "Hey, brother Parren, how ya doing?"

"Just fine. Where've you been?"

"Oh, I've been around." Then they'd say, "Hey, you think this Bakke thing is going to hurt me?"

And I would answer, "I hope it does. Because you've been sitting out there with your corporation and your nice spot; you've been ignoring other black people, and you're vulnerable."

All those folks who say, "We don't want certain classes of blacks in our neighborhoods," "We don't want our children to go to school where certain classes of blacks go"—they're just as vulnerable as we are. Look at Andrew Young. Here he was, a United Nations ambassador, and he lost his job. Even those who are government executives are vulnerable. They shouldn't suffer under the illusion that they can separate themselves from the masses of black people.

THOMAS: Still, some blacks want to divorce themselves from the black community. Are they what you call black Anglo-Saxons?

MITCHELL: The black Anglo-Saxon has come down through a series of definitions. At one time that person was called an Oreo cookie, black on the outside and white on the inside. Basically we're talking about people who simply don't know how to think from a black perspective. Instead of black Anglo-Saxon we should say Anglo-Saxon black, because this is the person who's afraid to use the word "black." He might use "minority," but he's scared to use "black." This is the person who's afraid to use a phrase like "white oppression." In other words, the black Anglo-Saxon just closes his or her mind to the reality of the present black experience and the reality of the black legacy.

THOMAS: Are any of these people present in the lower class rather than the middle or upper classes?

MITCHELL: Sure. Some of the most narrow-minded, selfish, nonblack blacks I've ever seen in my life are in the lower class. Some of them say, "There's that kid going to college and he doesn't need to go there, black folks made it without college."

THOMAS: Some people are suggesting that predominantly black institutions have no right to exist. Is that part of the strategy for containment?

MITCHELL: Sure it is. You can train an army and give it the best weapons and the best discipline, but if you round up all the generals, majors, lieutenants, and colonels, and kill them, who's going to lead the army? If you kill our black colleges, then you kill off the potential source of leadership in our black community. We get our leaders from our black churches and our black colleges and universities. To destroy, contain, or erode black institutions of higher learning is to diminish the potential for future leadership.

THOMAS: Yet some people are calling the elimination of predominantly black schools "desegregation," and they argue that desegregation is what blacks have been aiming for all these years.

MITCHELL: And black colleges and universities have been desegregated all of these years! I don't know of a single black college or university that doesn't admit whites. That has not been the problem. The problem has been the white institutions that didn't admit us. If black institutions say everybody is free to come, and nobody comes, then that's their business. I think the pressure for desegregation of the colleges ought not to fall on the black institutions.

We as a people don't have many things that we can claim. We can only claim our church, our institutions of higher learning, and a sense of racehood. That's about it. We can't claim wealth. Property. Political power. Economic power. It's enormously important that we hold onto that which we can claim.

THOMAS: What do we tell blacks who downtalk black colleges and churches? They fit right into the pattern set by whites of attacking black institutions.

MITCHELL: There are two angles to your question. Simply because we have a black institution, it doesn't mean that it's perfect; and therefore I welcome criticism of a black church or black college as long as it's positive and based on something real. But it's totally destructive to attack our institutions when you have no basis of fact. I've seen this happen all the time in the Congress. I've heard many congressmen stand up and say, "My black constituents wrote me and said the CETA program* is no good." That becomes a means of attacking something that's beneficial to us.

THOMAS: So history will record that the black person who wrote that letter in effect denied black people future jobs.

MITCHELL: Sure. And the power structure just loves that. They just love to parade out names of unthinking people who wrote, who sold out.

THOMAS: Congressman, according to Stephen Rosen in his book *Future Facts*, in the next few years, people will be able to get on trains, leave New York and end up in Los Angeles twenty-one minutes later—thirty-seven minutes if they want to stop off in Dallas. But blacks are not involved in planning for the future. Is this part of the containment strategy? For example, how do we fit into policy on genetic research? How do we fit into policy on heart or lung transplants? How do we fit into policy on control of the mind with drugs?

MITCHELL: Let me be very careful in answering you. Containment exists for only one purpose, and that is to maintain power where it is: away from black folks. Everything else you've talked about becomes ancillary to the basic thesis that power's got to stay where it is. We're not in on planning the

---

*The Comprehensive Employment Training Act (CETA) is a program to give job training to low-income unemployed people, by assisting the employer with funds to train and pay the employee.

high-speed railroads. It's all right for us to be a customer. That's powerlessness. But if we're in on it we might want to _buy_ the high-speed railroads. That's power, to be able to cut a line of transportation if we so desire. We're unable to be in on the latest advances in medicine. Medicine is an industry. It's a monopoly that excludes blacks. If we're in on that, then we might have the power to say, "We've developed the vaccine to stop this disease, but unless you do that which is right and positive for black people, we're not going to release it."

THOMAS: What are some examples of containment in the police department, and in the administration of "justice" in this country?

MITCHELL: I believe that in most police departments we have a deliberate effort to keep blacks at a lesser number, because police power is power, and we've got to be contained from sharing all of that power.

I believe that one of the big arguments against the all-voluntary army right now is that it's too black. More than a third of the standing army is black. That is access to power. Suppose America wanted to declare war on Zaire. Would those black troops fight black brothers? I hope they wouldn't. I suggest that's one of the reasons we're talking about going back to the draft. We have a fear that there are too many blacks in the military.

THOMAS: I've heard you speak on the dangers of a planned recession. What exactly do you mean?

MITCHELL: A planned recession in America takes place on two levels. One is through the federal reserve system, which controls the flow of money. If you've noticed, the federal reserve has tightened up on the flow of money. The money flow has dropped so suddenly it's off the chart. As a result, interest rates have gone up, prime rates are going up, and that's planning a recession.

Egyptian President Anwar Sadat meets with Parren Mitchell and other members of the Congressional Black Caucus (February, 1978). *(Wide World Photos)*

The other part of the plan is through fiscal policy. If the government cuts back drastically on what it puts into the economy, then you're planning for a recession. And that's exactly what has happened with this budget. We've cut a total of close to $14 billion out of the budget except for the military. That's how you plan a recession. The theory is that the only way to fight inflation is to slow down the economy, and that's crazy. In 1969 we balanced the budget and that's when the inflation rate doubled. I think a planned recession is a lie to the American people. It's not going to do anything for inflation.

THOMAS: What does it do?

MITCHELL: It shifts money so that the big money markets have access to money where we don't. General Motors can go through a planned recession because it has a sufficient capital reserve to keep itself in the prime spot. Ford can go through a planned recession. But you take the brother who's in business and hires ten people, he's got a little manufacturing plant, he doesn't have a reserve of capital to get through a planned recession.

THOMAS: In your political campaigns, what do you feel is the most important promise you've made—and kept—for the black community?

MITCHELL: There are really two. The night before I was first elected to Congress, a rally was held for me in a Jewish home; maybe two hundred people were there. The question was raised (and I'll never forget it), "What will your priorities be? Will you do more for blacks than for Jews or for whites?" My answer was, "I'll do something for everyone, but my priority is for black people. We need more, we hurt more, we have more pain." And a man who was there that night told me, "You will never get elected." I said, so be it. That was my commitment, which I have never broken, to prioritize for blacks.

My second commitment was to move us toward economic empowerment. I didn't know a thing about it. But when I got into Congress I learned. And that's been my major operation, economic empowerment for blacks. I have recently worked on the 10 percent set-aside and on Public Law 95–507, to give us some economic power so we can really get some political power.

THOMAS: Is there anything that will change the containment strategy? Do you feel we can, or should, move back to the sense of brotherhood we had in the sixties?

MITCHELL: We were together at one time and it shocked the devil out of America, that preachers and pimps and drunks and lawyers could all get out in the street together. That sense of unity scared white America. And white America started to work immediately to break it up, playing one group against another and manipulating one force against another. Now how do we put it back together? It's going to be a slow, tortuous process, and the first step in that process is to stop believing all the lies you are bombarded with every day by media other than the black media. We were divided because we listened to propaganda desiring to divide us.

The second step is for us to get back together on a small scale, and let that sense of togetherness grow. Let twelve people get together, call it a cadre, call it what you want, and say, "We are going to establish a covenant between us." Let that keep multiplying. We will get back our unity.

THOMAS: Congressman, we need you more than ever. Keep on playing Frederick Douglass and agitating, agitating, agitating. We need you because they have decided that they don't need us anymore. Thank you for "Like It Is."

June 17, 1980

MICHELE
WALLACE

BIOGRAPHY
MICHELE WALLACE

"I am saying, among other things, that for perhaps the last fifty years there has been a growing distrust, even hatred, between black men and women."

So says Michele Wallace in *Black Macho and the Myth of the Superwoman,* a startling and controversial book about blacks and the sexual politics of their experience in this country.

Ms. Wallace grew up during the sixties, when demonstrations and cries of "Black Power" were a part of daily life. At the age of seventeen she decided she would write a book about blacks and sexual politics. The result of almost ten years of researching and conducting interviews, *Black Macho and the Myth of the Superwoman* was published in February, 1979, by Dial Press. Wallace's conclusion, that "The black woman has become a social and intellectual suicide; the black man, unintrospective and oppressive," became the subject of intense debate. At the center of the debate are two devastating role models that limit blacks' perspective and their relationships: "Black Macho," and the "Superwoman."

Black Macho is the assertion of sexual power for its own sake. According to Ms. Wallace, the sixties quest for black manhood was simply an acting out of white male sexual fantasies about blacks. Instead of continuing to protect his family as he did during slavery, the black man ". . . risked everything—all the traditional goals of revolution: money, security, the overthrow of the government—in the pursuit of an immediate sense of his own power." The black man saw his universe as the whites defined it.

A victim of Black Macho is the black woman. She has her own stereotype:

[She is] a woman of inordinate strength, with an ability for tolerating an unusual amount of misery and heavy, distasteful work. This woman does not have the same fears, weaknesses, and insecurities as other women. . . . Less of a woman in that she is less "feminine" and helpless, she is really more of a woman in that she is the embodiment of Mother Earth, the quintessential mother with infinite sexual, life-giving, and nurturing reserves. In other words, she is a superwoman.

Instead of the powerful matriarch defined by myth, Ms. Wallace believes the black woman is actually the most vulnerable figure in American society. She is repudiated by her man, who, following white definitions, has decided she is not a "woman"; and she, looking at the American ideal of manhood, has concluded he is not a "man." For blacks, the move from slavery toward Americanization was a move toward self-hatred.

In addition to her book, which provoked discussion on important issues of the sixties and the present, Ms. Wallace has written articles for Esquire, The Village Voice, and Ms. The third generation of her family to grow up in Harlem, she attended the New Lincoln School, began her college education at Howard University, and later transferred to the City College of New York. She graduated with a B.A. in English and writing. From 1976 through 1978 she taught journalism at New York University. Currently on a leave of absence from that position, Ms. Wallace is at work on another book of nonfiction.

INTERVIEW
MICHELE WALLACE

ARTHUR THOMAS: Ms. Wallace, in your book, *Black Macho and the Myth of the Superwoman,* you argue that black sisters are no stronger than other women. But some people would argue that black women are in fact superwomen. The women in my life have truly been superwomen: a mother who refused to give up, a grandmother who refused to give up. I think about Harriet Tubman, I think about Sojourner Truth, I think about Ida B. Wells—dynamite sisters who did not quit, who had guts, who had courage, who had integrity. They made it possible for us to survive as a people. Is it a myth that sisters are superwomen?

MICHELE WALLACE: I think so. Black women have performed magnificently in the history of black people, but not more magnificently than would be indicated by the history of women in general. And although that may be disappointing and seems as if it's meant to take something away from black women, it isn't. It's a very important thing to understand in order for black women to advance and move where they need to be. What the black woman has done doesn't qualify her as a superwoman; she was merely acting as a responsible woman.

THOMAS: In some respects I understand what you're saying. I remember introducing psychiatrist Dr. Frances Cress Welsing, and I talked about her having the beauty of Lena Horne, the courage of Harriet Tubman, and the brilliance of Angela Davis. She said, "That's fine, but I want you to understand that I talk to women in my office every day, and they have, for four hundred years, had to bear a burden that they can't bear very much longer." Is that what you're saying in essence?

WALLACE: That's what I'm saying. It's important to understand that inability, because it does exist. Every Sojourner Truth was supported upon the accomplishments of many other black women, who were in turn supported upon the backs of many, many more black women—who died, who went crazy, who had sufferings they were not able to bear. It's great to have a Sojourner Truth. It's great to have a woman like your mother. But we won't continue to have strong women unless we treat them with more respect.

THOMAS: That's a key issue, respect. Stanley Elkins, in *Slavery: A Problem in American Institutional and Intellectual Life,* said that what happened to blacks during slavery also happened to people who were in German concentration camps. We looked at the slavemaster so long, we started seeing him as the father figure, or the figure in charge. Consequently, we started imitating him. Is this part of what happened, in your opinion, with black men in their relationship with black women? Did we start treating black women like we saw the slavemaster treating them?

WALLACE: I don't agree with what Elkins said, and Elkins, as a matter of fact, no longer agrees with what Elkins said. He recently renounced some of his earlier views about how severely manipulated and destroyed black people were psychologically.

THOMAS: Today though, black men in many instances disrespect black women. Is that somehow related to slavery? How did we treat each other then?

WALLACE: I don't think we disrespected each other during slavery. If we had, we wouldn't be here today. During slavery, despite the ways in which we were being indoctrinated by the slaveholders about how subhuman we were, we persisted in believing in, and in maintaining, a certain relationship between men and women, a certain respect.

THOMAS: Did the slaveholders in any way encourage black men to disrespect black women?

WALLACE: Yes. They encouraged disrespect simply by regarding black men and women as chattel, as animals that they were breeding. The purpose of men and women coming together was not marriage, or family, or anything like that. It was to breed offspring to sell in the market. That encouraged a disrespect for black women _and_ for black men.

THOMAS: Are you saying that while the black man was dehumanized, disrespected, discouraged, spat upon, kept from performing as a man in a man's world—that all those things did not force him to look down on the black woman during slavery? That the black man during slavery lived up to all that persecution and responded more positively to the needs of his family and his woman than he does today?

WALLACE: That's right. The slaves were at war. They knew it. And it was an announced, declared war. They knew their person was owned by people other than themselves. They knew that was wrong. They knew they were kept from worship. They knew they were kept from education. They had a very clear, definable problem. There was no confusion for them.

Today, we are confused. Some of us think we're actually free. Some of us think we can do what we want. Some of us think we're individuals. Some of us think we'd like to assimilate. Some of us think we can be as rich as we want to be. Some of us think we can ignore poor black people. There is a great deal of confusion about what we want to do, about what we should do, with our "freedom" and our rights. These are all points about which slaves, black people during slavery, were not confused. They didn't have any choices. They had to stick together, or they'd die!

THOMAS: I still have problems with what you call the "myth" of the superwoman. In your book, you described a sister who the slavemaster said could work well, she could do her job.

Michele Wallace speaking at Central State University about her book
Black Macho and the Myth of the Superwoman.

But this sister, when a white woman slapped her, beat the white woman out into the yard, knocked the white woman down, knocked the overseer down, knocked the slavemaster down, and told them all that she would not be beaten. And when they got ready to take her child, she threatened to kill the child to keep the child from staying with them. Now I know you have already separated the Sojourner Truths from those ladies whose names we don't even know. But I have to believe—

WALLACE: She was a superb woman!

THOMAS: I have to believe that, and I have to believe you see that superbness in every black woman on the face of this earth.

WALLACE: The strength you're pointing to is a human strength. It is not a black strength, it is not a woman's strength, it is not a black woman's strength. It is a human strength. That potential for strength, endurance, courage, inventiveness, and creativity exists in every human being God created. If it doesn't appear, it's because somebody's trifled with it. If you don't see that in young black men and women today to the extent that you think you ought to, which I don't, it's because it's been unduly trifled with.

THOMAS: Do you see that same quality in men?

WALLACE: It's there, it exists, but it's dormant. You cannot find more brilliant, more provocative, and more beautiful examples of courage and strength in black women than you can in the history of black men. For every black man who stood by and watched his wife get used sexually by another man—

THOMAS: A number of them died trying to stop that other man.

WALLACE: Exactly. People did impossible, unbelievable things. And we don't have the courage to do that today, with one-quarter of the obstacles.

THOMAS: In fact, we have been propagandized, and we have been victimized, into believing a battle existed between black men and black women during slavery.

WALLACE: Right.

THOMAS: We have been propagandized into believing a battle exists between us now, so that there, in fact, will be a battle and we will continue to dilute our collective power.

WALLACE: Right.

THOMAS: You contend that every human being has the mental strength black people have shown, and that white women could have borne the burden as black women did.

WALLACE: They have in other situations. I believe different cultures have different, unique, characteristic strengths. But there is a proud heritage of strength in the history of most people, if you look back far enough.

THOMAS: Do you feel black people didn't catch any more hell than anyone else?

WALLACE: Well, it's really very hard to say. When you look at history carefully, slavery wasn't born in America, suffering wasn't born there, useless and meaningless death was not born there, nor did it end there.

It was a brutal experience. But slavery was thousands of years old by the time black people came to America. Slavery existed in Africa, it existed in Asia. It was often cruel. It was often vicious. Servitude was a common human fate for masses of people. Beatings and corporal punishment were the order of the day throughout the world. I didn't mean to be a crusader about this particular point, but in my book I'm trying to say that the guideline establishing how slavery was conducted and the way black slaves were treated was not based upon thin air. It was based upon the way most poor people were treated. It was just a little bit lower.

THOMAS: We're still suffering the impact of that. No one can deny that the unemployment question of today, the drug question of today, any problem that we can come up with today, is somehow linked to that slavery period.

WALLACE: This is a valid point to debate. People disagree about it. I don't happen to think that our drug problem, our unemployment problem, et cetera, stem from the fact that we were enslaved. Slavery put us here before most other immigrant groups. Despite the obstacles that we had to overcome, there are no reasons without which, given equal opportunity, we could not have very much more than some of the other immigrant groups.

What has kept us where we are is that we *look different*. And therefore we can never become a part of this country. As long as this skin is black, we stand out. That was one of the things that kept us slaves. We couldn't hide, because we didn't look like other people.

THOMAS: W.E.B. DuBois said that no other woman possesses the loyalty, the femininity, the perceptivity, of the black woman.

WALLACE: I'm sorry, but I don't think that's true. I think it is reverse racism. Behind a superiority complex, there's always an inferiority complex.

THOMAS: I don't know if it was a superiority complex. I think he was trying to impress upon the men at that time the importance of respecting black women who were being disrespected by society. Now, Malcolm X in fact said the same thing: Respect the black woman. She is the mother of your children.

WALLACE: Of course. That is the basic thing, that men respect women because they are the mothers of their children, and that women respect men because they are the fathers of their children. To me, that's all that's required.

THOMAS: Are you implying that if a man respects the woman in a woman, that it is a feeling of superiority? How does one feel superior to one's lover? How does one feel superior to one's wife? How does one feel superior to one's sister? Is it a feeling of superiority toward the black woman when DuBois says, respect her, because nobody's more loyal than she is, nobody's more trustworthy, nobody's more feminine?

WALLACE: My finding is that, in the long run, when you deal with women in this way it is condescending. To remove women and say that they are better in certain respects is another way of removing women from the center of activity and saying, "Women are over there, they are on a pedestal, they're up in the clouds."

THOMAS: Are you saying that's the same thing the white man does, putting the white woman on a pedestal, and saying she's so good she can't come participate in the real world? All right, I understand what you're saying.

In your book you talk about the Black Power movement as an example of black brothers asserting their sexual power. What do you mean by that?

WALLACE: The civil rights movement was very oriented toward human goals. But certain manifestations of the Black Power movement, like cultural nationalism and the militancy of the Black Panthers, were unique to that period in the sense that there was a greater emphasis on the assertion of manhood as a goal, as opposed to an emphasis on human rights.

Now, it gets very complicated, because in one way the movement was well directed. Power does have to do with manhood in this world. If we're going to deal with political power, economic power, and the proper distribution of that power among black people, it's going to be among the men. That's the way things have been laid out in the past. You can't change everything at once.

But at the same time the emphasis on manhood created problems, because we couldn't afford the split it created between the sexes. Blacks have been the oppressed rather than the oppressors. We do not, and should not, function along the rules and the guidelines of the oppressor class, in this case, distributing all the power among the men. Functioning by the oppressors' rules is one of the ways of ensuring they'll always remain the oppressors.

THOMAS: In your book you state that the Black Panthers, the SNCC brothers, and the others who were involved in the movement didn't really have the interest of freeing black sisters at heart, but wanted to face the white man and come to grips with their own power. I have difficulty understanding or believing that the Black Panthers who were burned down by policemen in Chicago were only trying to prove their manhood.* I feel they were angry that their mothers, and grandmothers, and babies were being mistreated too, and that they had decided it was time to prove, "I'm a man, not only to me, but to my people." Is it possible that those young men who gave their lives for their people died not only with the interests of their manhood, but with the survival of their people at heart?

WALLACE: In my book I try to make a point about there being a difference, a complex difference, between ways of asserting manhood. I tell the story of Malcolm X, and I suggest that he was motivated by a struggle for manhood, and for him manhood meant providing for his women and his children, and protecting them. This is the traditional role of men. Malcolm X was fighting against not being able to provide for his family.

But I'm afraid that many of these men died. And I'm afraid that the fact that so many of them were killed

---

*On December 4, 1969, Cook County policemen in plainclothes raided Panther headquarters in Chicago. According to the police, they were searching for a cache of weapons on which they had an anonymous tip. They forced open a barricaded door and shooting ensued. After the battle ended, Illinois Panther Chairman Fred Hampton and Panther Mark Clark were dead.

motivated a lot of other people to take a much safer course, which was the pursuit of Black Macho.

THOMAS: What does today's black man have to do?

WALLACE: We must all do the same thing. Foremost, we must respect human rights. After that, we need a respect for our culture and our history, and we must respect the fact that each of us has a right to a certain amount of dignity and freedom. We must respect basic human needs: enough to eat, a place for shelter, and so forth. We must respect the space, in our history and culture, of each person.

Next, I think it's important to understand how fundamental, how central, family is to our society and to our future. When you respect that, and understand the need for that, then you respect men and women, and children, too.

THOMAS: The stereotypes you describe in your book seem to put black men and women at odds with each other. Do you see any hope for the constructive growth of relationships between black men and black women anytime in the near future?

WALLACE: I see and encourage every possibility for the future of black men and women together. Men and women can't exist apart. We have gotten as far apart as we can possibly be. We're much more dependent upon each other than we even realize.

THOMAS: I hope that your book will make it possible for black men and women to live, love, trust, respect, and work cooperatively together. Thank you for "Like It Is."

January 1, 1980

JERRY
PAUL

BIOGRAPHY
JERRY PAUL

Jerry Paul, Attorney at Law, opened his own civil rights law firm in Greenville, North Carolina, in 1968. In the early days of his practice he often traded legal services for meals and a place to sleep. During his first year he defended in more than forty cases, with each one ending in acquittal for his client. Since then, Mr. Paul's clients have included Joan Little, Delbert Tibbs, the Black Panther Party of North Carolina, the North Carolina Civil Liberties Defense Fund, the Pitt County NAACP, Dr. Ralph Abernathy, and the National Tenant's Organization.

In 1974 Mr. Paul became a lawyer for Joan (pronounced JoAnne) Little, a black woman charged with first degree murder for the stabbing death of her white jailer, Clarence Alligood. Alligood was found dead in Little's cell in the Beaufort County, North Carolina, jail, his body stabbed with an ice pick. The pick lay in his right hand, his left hand clutched at his trousers. Except for a pair of socks, Alligood was naked from the waist down. Little, who surrendered to authorities a week later, admitted she killed Alligood, but said she killed him in self-defense. She claimed the jailer had forced her to perform oral sex as he held the ice pick to her face.

Paul, working with lawyer Karen Galloway, spent over eleven months planning Little's legal strategy. That strategy included importing a high-powered team of legal specialists and using scientific jury selection methods, social science techniques, and videotape preparation of witnesses for the defense. His modern strategies were clearly successful. The jury of six blacks and six whites took only seventy-eight minutes to decide that the prosecution had not proved Miss Little guilty. She was acquitted of murder.

Paul later gained a certain amount of notoriety for claiming the Joan Little trial was a charade. He said he "bought" Miss

Little's acquittal with the $325,000 used to mount an extensive jury selection process, to fly in expert witnesses, to counsel Miss Little in preparation for her testimony, and to hire investigators. Paul denounced the justice system as a farce, claiming that orchestrating the press was more powerful than justice in proving innocence or guilt.

Paul's outspoken attacks on the justice system underline a personal philosophy. At the end of the Joan Little trial he said:

> I've spent a long time in this state fighting for social change, and sometimes I do become emotional and outspoken and heated. That heat is not hatred, and it is not spoken in anger to belittle anyone or to hurt anyone. Sometimes it is necessary that we speak out, knowing that others will become angry at us, so that a thought process will result in growth.*

Mr. Paul is a member of the National Lawyers Guild and the American Bar Association. He is a board member of the North Carolina Civil Liberties Union, the North Carolina chapter of the Southern Christian Leadership Conference, and both the North Carolina and National Chapters of the Alliance against Racist and Political Repression. Mr. Paul currently practices law in the state of New York, and teaches a course at the City College of New York on the legal history of the Southern civil rights movement.

---

*Quoted in James Reston, Jr., *The Innocence of Joan Little* (New York: Times Books, 1977), pp. 325–6.

INTERVIEW
JERRY PAUL

ARTHUR THOMAS: Jerry, what was a southern judge's definition of a shame?

JERRY PAUL: Before the second Joan Little trial started, the state trial, the trial judge talked to the members of the press at a press conference and he asked them, "Do you all know what a shame is?" They of course said no. He said, "A shame is a busload of niggers going over a cliff with an empty seat." And the trial started with that comment.

    The press would not report that he had made that statement, because they said the editors wouldn't print it. That attitude shows the failure of the press to deal with issues in this country. And it shows the underlying current that is becoming even more prevalent in this country. The racists now feel they can be more outspoken, they can do more. Several years ago when there was a gas crisis in this country, I was sitting outside a judge's chambers and he'd forgotten and left the door open. He and three or four lawyers were sitting around talking, and one made the comment that we would not now have a gas crisis if Hitler had been allowed to finish his work in the world. And the judge agreed with him.

THOMAS: These judges—a judge with that definition of a shame, a judge promoting Hitler—these same judges are passing judgment on black folks and on Jewish people and on the poor and the oppressed. How can you, as an attorney, advocate that we still use this legal system?

PAUL: I personally don't advocate using this legal system, but many lawyers do. I think they recognize—more of them, I think, than are willing to say so—that a legal system with

1975: Joan Little (center) and her attorney, Jerry Paul (right), leave the courthouse where Paul is arguing to get her murder indictment quashed. *(Wide World Photos)*

those attitudes best serves their interests. They like where they are. They like the fact that they are in power. In a revolutionary society perhaps we wouldn't need lawyers, or not need lawyers in the same way we do in this society.

THOMAS: Jerry, it appears to me that, as a lawyer, if the judge getting ready to try one of your clients makes a statement like that definition of shame, haven't you got grounds for not using that judge, or for having him disrobed?

PAUL: It would appear so, but that is not the case. Often we are tempted to get rid of judges for those reasons, but the judiciary and the legislature and the people who are in control will not do anything about it. This particular judge has done many things like that. In fact, during a murder case in which a person was being tried for the death penalty, while the jury was being picked, the judge took some paper and constructed a paper noose, which he was swinging from the desk. And I've seen much worse.

THOMAS: You were trial attorney for Joan Little, a black North Carolina woman indicted for first degree murder after she killed a prison guard. You stated that Clarence Alligood, the prison guard, would never have been charged with first degree murder if Joan Little had been found stabbed to death in his office. Joan Little is black and female. Clarence Alligood was white and male. That is the political issue. What were you talking about when you said that?

PAUL: Joan was not being tried for factual setting, but she was being tried because of prejudice and assumptions. The judicial system and the white people who control the judicial system all assumed that since she was black, and since she was a female, that she must be a prostitute, she must be a liar, and she must be a murderer. And no matter what the facts said, they assumed she did something wrong. They knew it couldn't have happened any other way than if she was guilty. She was not tried because facts and circumstances showed her to be guilty, but she was tried because she was a woman and a black woman.

THOMAS: Was she a political prisoner?

PAUL: She was a political prisoner because she was being tried for her sex and the color of her skin, and she was being tried to reinforce the attitudes of the white community. They wanted to prove that black people and black women are criminals. They wanted to prove that no police officer— remember, this was a police officer who was killed—would do anything wrong. If it is proven in court that police officers do things wrong, then the power structure is threatened.

THOMAS: Are there any other political prisoners in this society?

PAUL: There are many political prisoners in this country. Ben

Chavis, George Merritt, David Poindexter, David Johnson—I could go on and on. The United Nations Committee of International Juries studied the situation in this country this summer and found that there were political prisoners in the United States. In fact there were more political prisoners in the United States than there are in many of the countries the United States complains about.

THOMAS: Is there a dual system of justice in this country? One for the poor and one for the rich, one for blacks and one for whites?

PAUL: Yes, there is. The bar attempted to disbar me for saying that. I made several statements. I said the judicial system is racist, I said that I am a freedom fighter, and I said there are two types of justice in this country, one for the rich and one for the poor. They then charged me with violating the canon of ethics, with casting dispersions upon the judicial system, and they attempted to disbar me.

Shortly after that Patty Hearst was pardoned. In California an old senator and onetime president of San Francisco State, along with a few other people who were in control of this country, tried for her release and she was released. Ben Chavis, a freedom fighter in North Carolina, was still in jail. The world has cried for his release. It falls on deaf ears.*

THOMAS: What can be done to eliminate the dual justice system in this country?

PAUL: You have to eliminate the economic disparities. Any time you talk about any facet of this society, whether it be judicial or medical or whatever, you keep running into problems when you only concern yourself with the forms. In the final analysis something has to be done about our economic

---

*Civil rights activist Ben Chavis and nine other defendants were charged with arson and conspiracy following racial violence at Wilmington, North Carolina, in 1971. They are known as the Wilmington 10.

system. We can no longer tolerate one person having three or four houses and driving six cars while some people don't even have one room to live in.

THOMAS: Are poor people really the criminals in this country?

PAUL: No. If you define criminal acts as acts that are antisocial, harmful to oneself and others, rich people commit more crimes than poor people do. Placing the blame for crime on poor people is an attempt to blame the victims. It is an attempt to divert the true issue, to put it in a light that lets rich people be paternalistic.

Crimes are committed by rich people. If you look at the three largest corporations in this country, you find that they have been convicted an average of three times in the last twenty-five years of major felonies. Yet these people are not in jail. In San Diego a while back a bank was robbed and three young men stole $15,000. They were caught and sentenced to twenty-five years in jail. When an audit was done of the bank because of the robbery, they discovered the bank president had embezzled funds of almost a half-million dollars. He got five years probation and a hundred-dollar fine. When people see these things happening, they don't respond to this unequal justice.

THOMAS: I often speak in prisons. When I get finished giving a speech, every youngster who comes up to me will say, "Dr. Thomas, I was innocent; I did not do it." I have not in the past ten years come into contact with one individual in prison who actually told me that he was guilty. Are we really treated that unjustly, or are some of the brothers just rapping?

PAUL: The police have found themselves in a sacred position in society between the American flag and apple pie. They have decided, and it happens in case after case, that they can lie about the evidence, they can destroy evidence that is in the defendant's favor, they can say there was a confession when there was no confession. And the judges permit this because they always believe the police. Because of that, convictions are gained illegally. Sometimes a person is guilty, but the police cheated to convict that person. People find it distasteful when that happens and they maintain their innocence, as they should. Their guilt was not proved fairly.

The focus on poor people who are victims and the absolute faith that is put in policemen is an attempt to make the issues unclear and to divert the attention from where the attention ought to be. The attention ought to be on the real criminals in this country, those who are really responsible for crime: the corporations, the people that run the government.

THOMAS: Are there attempts to organize in prisons as far as the Ku Klux Klan is concerned?

PAUL: Yes. Since 1970 the Klan has been organizing in the North and they have concentrated on the prison guards, because they noted that a lot of the liberation struggle is going on around the prisons. They felt the best way to combat that was to organize the prison guards. With the help of the ACLU they were permitted to organize in the prisons. At the Eastern New York Correctional Facility in Napanoch, New York, the Klan instigated a riot which was basically a fight between the Klan guards and the prisoners trying to protect themselves from the Klan guards. After the riot the State indicted the prisoners. One of the charges against the prisoners was coercion, because the prisoners had signed a petition calling for better food and asking that the Klan guards who had beaten up some prisoners be fired.

THOMAS: So in effect the State took the Klan's position. The State defended the Klan.*

---

*The riot took place in Napanoch on August 8, 1977. On September 3 of that year, the State Correctional Services Commissioner in New York issued a directive prohibiting employees of the prison system from belonging to the Ku Klux Klan.

In North Carolina you grew up around obvious preju-
dices and stereotyped attitudes and yet you are, in my
opinion, a great champion of justice, equality, and humanity. What moved you to risk your life against the Klan or to
sometimes be disregarded by your family?

PAUL: I don't like inhumanity, I don't like miscarriages of justice,
I don't like one group of people treating another group of
people wrong simply because they have the power to do so. I
know that I have a high regard for my own freedom. I think
that everybody ought to have that same freedom. And I
know that I can best protect my freedom by protecting other
people's.

I would like to be at the rhythm of society where we
could enjoy life and where the important things, such as the
quality of life, mean something. This won't come until we
do something about the state of freedom and about the state
of justice.

THOMAS: More specifically, you have had to make decisions,
even in regard to your parents, about the social issues you
are confronted with. This is something that obviously
developed over a period of time. At one point in your
childhood you ate out on the porch for a week because you
felt something your parents had done was not right. What
happened to you from the time you made the stand against
your parents?

PAUL: You're talking about the time a black man who had worked
for my father came to our house, and I asked him to eat
breakfast with us. My parents told me that he could not do
so, because he was black. At that point I told my parents, "If
he can't eat here, then I can't either." So I went out on the
porch and I ate there, and I refused to come back to the table
until they changed their policies. I did that because I was
angry at the way they treated another human being.

THOMAS: How old were you?

PAUL: I was ten or eleven years old.

THOMAS: Your environment didn't tell you to do that. What made you do it?

PAUL: I'm not sure. I do know that I was often in the position of being a rebel and of speaking out. I am just not going to put up with anyone treating people wrong—not when I can do something about it. Not when they are wrongs that I can help.

   I would like to relate the story of a German war bride who lived as a child in Germany during World War II. She married an American soldier. She tried to emigrate to this country and they asked her a question: Do you understand mass guilt? She didn't give the right answer, so they didn't allow her to emigrate. Later on she reapplied and came to this country. At a point during the Vietnam war, this woman dressed up in her Sunday clothes, put on her white gloves, and went down to where they were loading napalm bombs onto boats heading for Vietnam. She lay down in front of the trucks that were loading the napalm bombs. She was arrested and thrown in jail. And they asked her, "Why did you do this? You are a middle-class person, dressed up all fine." She said, "Sir, when the question in later years comes to my children, 'Where were your parents when . . .?' they won't have to stand by in embarrassed silence, because today I cast my vote for freedom and I lay down in front of the truck."

   That always has impressed me. And I can't live otherwise. I have to deal with those questions. And if you ask me how to cast my vote, I am going to cast it for freedom. No matter what the consequences.

THOMAS: That attitude was more common during the sixties. What has happened to the movement since then?

PAUL: The movement of the sixties has been destroyed by the press and by those who say the problems are different today, that improvements have been made. Too few people now are willing to speak out and struggle. But the problem is still there. The organization I belong to, the National Alliance against Racist and Political Repression, has a heavier caseload this year than we have ever had.

THOMAS: Was one of our problems with the civil rights movement that we didn't set up a system to protect it?

PAUL: During the sixties we believed that the change would be permanent. We believed in the goodness of the people. We did not understand that the liberals were going to desert us as they did. We did not understand that the moderates were going to fail. We did not set up ways and act to defend the gains we had made. And then we ran off to other issues.

This country and the people in this country made a commitment to end racism during the sixties. The first time other issues appeared—environmental rights, women's liberation, all those things—people ran to those issues and stopped dealing with racism. We are going to have to go back and say, "You didn't solve the problem of racism. You made that commitment and we won't rest until that commitment is fulfilled."

THOMAS: What did you learn from the Joan Little case?

PAUL: I was able to refine and develop some new trial techniques that are now put into practice more often in this country, for instance, jury selection techniques. I also learned how the courts aid the government in distorting the issues. After the Joan Little case they wanted to claim she had a fair trial. "Look how good we were to her, we freed her. We gave her a fair trial. How could this be such a bad system if Joan Little was freed?"

Well, they didn't give her anything. We fought for her freedom. We forced them into every issue. We forced everything that we got out of them. And when you have to spend, as we did, $300,000 to get an innocent person free—that's too much. That is too great a price to pay. When I saw that woman destroyed by the prison, when I saw her life wrecked, when I saw all the pressure she was under and all the pressure the people who worked on the defense committee were under, all the sacrifice—that's asking too much.

THOMAS: Did the Joan Little case in any way develop within the hearts and minds of black America a better appreciation and respect for black women? White racist jailers aren't the only ones who disrespect black women.

PAUL: I think it did. From campuses I've spoken on and people I've talked to and articles I've read, I think that the courage of black women became a point of dialogue. People began to talk about the courage of black women and what black women have suffered through in this country. From the talk about what happened to Joan, black women became more aware of their own heritage, and other people became aware of the sacrifices and the great courage with which black women have acted throughout history.

THOMAS: What is Ms. Little doing now?

PAUL: She is working in the National Council of Black Lawyers office.

THOMAS: Do you see any social danger in encouraging young people to disrespect the law?

PAUL: I think that is a very healthy thing to do. In fact, had young people not been encouraged to disrespect the law, black people would still be riding in the back of the bus. Black people would still be eating at separate lunch counters. If disrespect for the law had not been encouraged, we'd be flying a British flag today. It is healthy for a democracy in any country not to have sacred images, because once an image is sacred, the people can't question it. Then tyranny exists.

THOMAS: How can poor people find out about legal assistance if they have been unjustly convicted?

PAUL: There are several ways. They can contact the public defender. They can contact legal aid agencies. There are several national organizations they can contact for lawyers' names. I don't mean to imply that people should always depend on lawyers, because there are many nonlawyer legal workers who do a lot to help people achieve justice. There are publications that contain the names and addresses of organizations in this country that can help. One publication can be obtained from the Committee for Racial Justice of the United Church of Christ, and one can be obtained from the National Alliance Against Racist and Political Repression.

THOMAS: Mr. Paul, for your sense of justice and for your work to make justice a reality, thank you for "Like It Is."

November 20, 1979

JULIAN BOND

BIOGRAPHY
JULIAN BOND

Julian Bond, Georgia State Senator, began his political career in 1965 when he was elected to the Georgia House of Representatives. He and five other blacks who won House seats in that election where the first blacks to sit in the Georgia House since 1907. Bond catapulted to national prominence at the 1968 Democratic Convention when he became the first black ever nominated for the vice-presidency of the United States.

He comes from a scholarly background—his father, a leading educator, was president of Lincoln College. Bond attended Chestnut Grove High School and The George School, a Quaker preparatory school in northeastern Pennsylvania.

At Morehouse College in Atlanta, he became active in the civil rights movement in the South. He helped found the Committee on Appeal for Human Rights (COAHR), and became their communications director, writing position papers, letters, news releases, and other publicity releases. In 1960, the organization merged into SNCC, the Student Non-Violent Coordinating Committee.

SNCC was strongly involved in voter registration. Following the Federal Voting Rights Act of 1965 and reapportionment of voting districts in the South, it became more feasible for blacks to run for public office. Bond ran for the State House of Representatives in 1965, and won with 82 percent of the vote. The Georgia House, objecting to his statements about the Vietnam war, attempted to bar Bond from taking office, but he was granted his seat on an appeal to the Supreme Court.

In 1968, Bond was cochairman of the insurgent delegation that successfully unseated the regular Georgia delegation to the Democratic Convention. The challenge delegation, composed of the blacks and liberals conspicuously absent from Governor Lester Maddox's delegation, won one-half of the state's forty-two allotted seats. A move began to nominate Bond for the vice-presidency. He received forty-eight and a half votes before announcing, "I deeply appreciate the honor, but unfortunately I have not yet reached the age and must therefore ask that my name be removed." Bond was twenty-eight at the time.

Bond continues to base his political activities in Georgia. Elected to the Georgia State Senate in 1974, he presently concentrates on voter organization, and is chairman of the Southern Elections Fund (SEF). The SEF supplies money and technical assistance to southern blacks seeking political office. Since its inception in 1969, the fund has helped elect over four hundred black candidates.

In addition to his work in the state senate and with the SEF, Bond is president of the Southern Poverty Law Center, president of the Atlanta NAACP and a member of the National Board of the NAACP, and a member of the New Democratic Coalition and Voter Education Fund.

INTERVIEW
JULIAN BOND

THOMAS: Mr. Bond, are conditions ripe for another revolution in this country?

JULIAN BOND: They're certainly ripe for another series of explosions. Whether or not those explosions become a revolution is another question. But when you look at unemployment in the black community and the proposed budget cuts now being considered by the President and by Congress, when you realize that the rate of inflation hits the people who have the least amount of money the hardest, and when you imagine that a long, hot summer is about to come up when you'll have thousands of young black men and women in the streets—idle, unemployed, no prospects for a job—that's a prescription for an explosion. All it takes is some heavy-handed action by some policeman somewhere, and a rumor through the crowd, and Boom! There goes another city.

THOMAS: Has this country decided, politically and psychologically, that blacks are no longer important and that they should simply be written off?

BOND: I think a large portion of the country has made that decision. Look at the Congress now. Out of 435 members of the U.S. House of Representatives, only about 80 members can be counted on as continual friends of black and poor people. There are only about 80 out of 435 who can be counted on to consistently vote for the kinds of assistance programs, affirmative action programs, and other government programs that help people at the bottom end of the economic ladder.

At the same time, I think it's important to note that we have, in a peculiar way, almost volunteered for this position. We don't register to vote. Those of us who are registered don't vote in large numbers. We're not as attentive as we ought to be to current affairs, to what's going on in the world about us. So it's a peculiar mix of having the country decide we're expendable, and having a great many of us decide we're expendable, too.

THOMAS: Then Samuel Yette's book, *The Choice: The Issue of Black Survival in America*, is a real possibility—America has decided it doesn't need blacks anymore.

BOND: Very real. It's almost as though he knew this period was coming. He predicted it very accurately. The real question is, how are we going to respond? Will we wait for America to say, "We didn't mean it, we're going to treat you better"? Or will we begin to stand up and *insist* that we be treated better?

THOMAS: We insisted during the sixties that there be some changes, but we aren't as vocal now. What were the accomplishments of the university students of the sixties, and of the seventies? What do the students of the eighties have to do?

BOND: The eighties are a question mark. We don't know what these young people are going to do. So far, we see them opposing the President's call for a resumption of the draft, but we don't know if it's because they personally do not want to go, or because they think the draft as an instrument of foreign policy is incorrect. We don't know if this is part of the 1970s selfishness or a revival of the 1960s feeling of community, of caring.

The sixties students lived in a very different time from now. And they behaved in a very different way. They determined that they had within themselves the ability to effect some change in society. They could integrate lunch counters. *They* could integrate movie theaters. *They* could register voters. *They* could change the course of American history, and change it they did. In the 1970s there began to be a winding down. Instead of being interested in the large picture, young people began to be interested in the university itself, in reforming the college, in fighting for changes in rules and procedures within the academic institution. Toward the end of that decade the picture got still narrower and students seemed to be interested primarily in themselves. You see enormous interest in astrology; people find out who they are by reading the newspaper. You find tremendous interest in exotic diet and odd religions. It's a period of looking at your own navel.

Now whether or not that's going to change in the eighties, I don't know. We've put a lot of hope in these young people. I believe the hope is going to be delivered, and that we're going to be proud of them in the next ten years.

THOMAS: Lerone Bennett says young blacks today lack a sense of being able to identify white racism, a sense of knowing when a white person is either deliberately or subconsciously trying to run a game on them. Do you see this in your travels? If this condition does exist, how do we deal with it? How do we deal with a generation of young blacks who don't recognize white racism?

BOND: I see that every place I go. A few days ago I was in Mississippi, and I stood on the banks of the Tallahachee River, where Emmett Till's body had been thrown in 1955. And the thought struck me that even though that kind of lynching does not occur with any great regularity anymore, a different kind of lynching of young black people occurs almost every day. Unemployment rates for young black men are four times the national average. A young black man with a college degree is on the average going to make only $110 more a year than a white boy with a high school diploma.

Julian Bond withdraws his name from consideration as a Vice Presidential candidate after it was entered in nomination at the Democratic National Convention, 1968. *(Wide World Photos)*

Now if that's not sufficient motivation for young people to register to vote, to become interested in their community, to join the NAACP, to involve themselves in the hundreds and hundreds of worthwhile projects that do exist and need to exist in the American black community, I don't know what is. I hope we don't have to go back to the day when there were signs that said "white" and "colored," when white people were universally racist—I hope it doesn't take that to wake this generation of young black people up. They seem to me to be coasting through life. They're going to find, however, that there's an uncomfortable drop at the end of *this* roller coaster.

THOMAS: I heard a former high-level federal official say that America hasn't really decided what it wants to do with black people. It hasn't decided whether it wants to integrate us, annihilate us, or desegregate us. What are your views on that?

BOND: That's an accurate assessment. There is confusion in state governments and in the federal government about what exactly ought to be done with this group of people, this 13 percent of the population that is black. At the same time, again, there's confusion among us. Young people especially seem to have no interest in their own future, in the economic or physical safety and security of their community. They have no concern about the kind of education they received and their younger brothers and sisters will be receiving. And that's a tragic, tragic circumstance.

THOMAS: In spite of high unemployment among black people, we're facing major federal budget cuts in social services and education. What is the effect likely to be?

BOND: If the budget cuts are successful, they're going to be awfully damaging to poor people generally in the United States, and particularly to black people, too many of whom are poor. There's only one defense against them, and that's a political defense. We are like soldiers going onto the battlefield leaving half our army home. Because blacks are not registered or don't vote, we can't expect to win.

THOMAS: Why don't we register as we should in the numbers that we should, and why don't we vote?

BOND: I think it's because we don't understand the connection between the vote, the deciding of public policy, and our own lives. A candidate runs for mayor of Anytown, U.S.A. That candidate says, "If you vote for me I'm going to see that a, b, and c is done." We turn out and vote for him in large numbers; he wins the election, and instead of doing a, b, and c, he only does a. We are so easily turned off that we say, "I'll never vote again. This man disappointed me. I'll never vote again."

Then, we don't understand the mathematics of the political process. I meet people who say, "I've only got this one vote, what difference does it make?" You know, Adolf Hitler was elected German chancellor by one vote. One vote would have made the difference in a World War and the deaths of millions and millions of people and the whole course of human history.

But young people don't see the connection. Unless they see some immediate, personal, material benefit in any kind of political action, they won't do it. I've asked young people in my own city to join the NAACP and the first thing they say is, "What's in it for me?" As though this were some kind of lottery with a prize at the end, a trip to Bermuda for the weekend.

THOMAS: Where do they learn this attitude?

BOND: They absorb it from the world about them. Once they've absorbed it, they don't unlearn it because they are not told in school the conditions black people face in America today, or the conditions black people faced in America yesterday. And they aren't shown the connection between militant action and an improvement of those conditions.

THOMAS: How important are black colleges to the survival of black people? Many people think that they only have an educational mission.

BOND: More than 50 percent of black young people go to predominantly white schools, but predominantly black schools graduate the majority of black young people who get a bachelor of arts degree.

THOMAS: So 105 schools do a better job for blacks than 3,000.

BOND: Exactly so. We are swooping into the white colleges in large numbers, but we're not coming out the other end. We're instead graduating from Morehouse College, from Central State University, from black colleges all over the country. We have to remind ourselves that Thurgood Marshall did not go to Harvard, that Stokely Carmichael did not go to the University of Pennsylvania, that Maynard Jackson, the mayor of Atlanta, did not go to the University of Georgia. These men and dozens of other men and women—who are doctors, lawyers, dentists, judges, politicians, policemen, business executives, and educators—went to black colleges.

THOMAS: And yet there are black counselors, black principals, and black professionals who attended black colleges and who now sit in a middle-class suburb and will say point-blank to a student, "Don't go to a black school. You have a better chance in a historically white university. You're going to get a better job. You're going to get a better education." Is it important that we deal directly with the image blacks have of the black colleges and universities?

BOND: I think you have to deal with it and you have to deal with those people. I went to Morehouse College. My college has produced more black doctors than any other school in the United States. More black doctors got their undergraduate training at my school than at any other school in the country. That's a proud record, and it's a record that's going to be repeated over and over and over again, because around the country there are young people who know that if they want a good premed education, Morehouse College is the place to go. So we've got to say, not only to this class of young people who are about to come into these schools, but also to their alumni, and to those black professional people who could not or did not go to a black school, that here is a valuable resource. We can't exist without this resource. We must build it up. We must contribute to it. Alumni must give, nonalumni must give, we must get corporate America to give, we must get public and private sources to give. We must make sure these schools are as good and as strong as they possibly can be, because their strength is our strength.

THOMAS: What role do you think black universities and colleges play in building up students' political awareness? Do you feel they are performing adequately?

BOND: I think the universities perform well. As far as I can see, they are basically doing today what they did in an earlier period when the students were much more involved. A couple of things have changed. The general atmosphere in the country has changed. In many ways we are Americans too, and we reflect the general attitude in the United States. When others in the United States withdraw into themselves, we do the same thing. When others in the United States become self-centered, we do the same thing.

The difference is, we can't afford it. It's a luxury for them. It's a tragic mistake for us.

I don't think the fault lies in the university, although there is no institution in America that does what it could do and what it should do to help solve this problem. I think the reason for student apathy lies in the times, in the nature of the education younger people are receiving earlier on the educational ladder, and in the students themselves.

THOMAS: Where are we going with resumption of the draft? How does it relate to black people?

BOND: I represent four black college campuses: Morehouse, Spellman, Clark, and Morris Brown. As far as I know, they haven't said a peep about the draft. And they're likely to be the first ones to go.

THOMAS: What do you tell young black men who think the only way they can prove their manhood is to join the army and then volunteer for the paratroopers, to join the Marine Corps so they can be the first one on the beach? We have a responsibility to our community, not just our country. What do you tell them when you compound the possibility of casualties in war with the fact that there are a million more black women in this country than black men?

BOND: That macho image of a man is old-fashioned. I'd hope that a man in this country isn't measured by the circumference of his biceps, but by the activity of his brain, not in his ability to beat someone up, but in his ability to build something up.

THOMAS: On the other hand, we have youngsters who are unemployed, who have no place to go except perhaps a jail cell. Where do they draw the line between volunteering for the army and remaining unemployed, staying in the street?

BOND: Under a certain set of circumstances, I think a military career can be exciting, entertaining, and educational for black young people. I'm impressed by the number of young black women I meet who are going into the military, now that career opportunities are open for them there that weren't open to women five or ten years ago. Depending upon the terms of their enrollment, they get a chance at completion of a high school eduation, the chance to learn a skill, a trade, a career. And I don't at all object to that. In fact, I would encourage some young people to go in that direction. I do object, however, to the guy who thinks that in order to be Mr. Macho he's got to have a gun in hand with a bayonet stuck on the end, and he has to kill the first person he sees.

THOMAS: John Conyers* said there could be a black president in the next twenty years. Do you agree with that?

BOND: I agree. I think there could be. I'll tell you what it takes. First of all, it takes for all of us to register to vote. Second, it takes for us to develop a candidate who can appeal not only to us but to the white electorate as well. And finally it takes our ability, which I think we have now, to finance such a

---

*John Conyers is a black Congressman from Detroit, Michigan.

campaign. That's awfully important. I tried to run for president in a small way as a protest in 1972. I raised $13,000. You can't be elected mayor of a medium-sized town for $13,000.

But there is money in the American black community and there is money in the American white community that would go to such a candidate. It's entirely possible that within the next two decades you're going to see a black man or woman making a decent race for the presidency of the United States. Now perhaps he or she won't win, but I think you're going to see some black person making an honest, straightforward, well-financed, well-organized race. And if he or she doesn't win, it will be less because of the color of his or her skin than because of the difficulties of being all things to this peculiar American electorate.

THOMAS: Moving toward our goal of a black president, what should our party affiliation be? Do we stick with one party? Do we get in both parties? Or do we form our own party?

BOND: Well, we can't form our own if it's composed only of blacks. We are 13 percent of the population, and 13 percent has never won an election. Now, 13 percent plus some other percent can win an election, but as long as it's only us, it's a losing proposition.

I think we ought to be able to be either Democrats or Republicans. We have traditionally voted for Democrats. In most presidential elections over the last twenty years the Democratic candidate has been better for us than the Republican candidate. But that won't always be the case. It may not be the case in the election in 1984, in 1988, in 1992, and so on. We have to be flexible enough to shift.

On the local level, particularly in state and municipal politics, I think we've got to follow an even more independent course. We have to get out good candidates from *both* parties by voting in the primaries. We have to say, some of us are going to vote for this Republican who's pretty good, and the rest of us are going to stay over here with the

Democrats. When we come down to a choice between two good people, then we can choose one of those two. But it's a foolish, foolish mistake for us to be yellow-dog Democrats, and to vote for a yellow-dog candidate simply because he is nominated by the Democratic party.

THOMAS: What kind of leadership style do you think is going to appear in the eighties?

BOND: I think what we need is leadership that does not necessarily say, "Follow me," but leadership that says, "Here are the facts, they are undeniable. Here are several solutions to the problem. Choose one of them and do something about it. You may not choose the one I've chosen, but at least do something about it." That's the kind of leadership we're likely to see.

Additionally, I think we're going to see an increasing number of specialists. In the early sixties, black leadership was basically generalist leadership. Martin Luther King, for example, was the great generalist. If your problem was police brutality, Dr. King had a solution. If your problem was bad housing, Dr. King had a solution. If your problem was any of the separate problems black people face under white racism in the United States, Dr. King had a solution. We're going to see more people who will say, "My interest and expertise is in housing. Some black people face poor housing, and I've got something for that. If, on the other hand, the problem is police brutality, this fellow here is the expert on that. He's the trained person. He's educated. He's skilled in this field." We're going to develop a range of specialists, and on the whole I think we'll be better served in that fashion.

THOMAS: Brother, we thank you very much for your many contributions to the survival of all people. You're a great man. It's a pleasure to be with you. Thank you for "Like It Is."

May 6, 1980

JESSE JACKSON

BIOGRAPHY
JESSE JACKSON

Reverend Jesse Louis Jackson calls himself "The Country Preacher," but his high-powered message is especially effective in reaching city students and leaders. Jackson, who has emerged as a likely heir to the civil rights leadership of Dr. Martin Luther King, Jr., preaches King's message of hope and nonviolent change in a revved-up street style that has been called a combination of southern revival meeting and razzle-dazzle. His message: Blacks need to muster the will to close educational and economic gaps that exist in our society.

Jesse Jackson was born October 8, 1941, in Greenville, South Carolina. At Greenville's all-black Sterling High School he starred in football, basketball, and baseball. The Chicago White Sox made a bid for Jackson, but he declined the baseball contract and accepted an athletic scholarship to the University of Illinois. After a coach at Illinois informed him that, ability notwithstanding, blacks were linemen and not quarterbacks on the university football team, he transferred to North Carolina Agricultural and Technical College.

At North Carolina A & T, Jackson's talent for protest and leadership first emerged. As leader of the student sit-in campaign, he headed the daily marches and sit-ins that broke the color line in downtown Greensboro's restaurants, movie theaters, and other public facilities. In recognition of his work he was elected president of the newly formed North Carolina Intercollegiate Council on Human Rights. In his senior year, Jackson became involved with CORE, the Congress of Racial Equality. He was later named field director of CORE's Southeastern Operations. After graduating in 1964 with a degree in sociology, Jackson accepted a Rockefeller Foundation grant to study at the Chicago Theological Seminary.

In 1966 the Southern Christian Leadership Conference

(SCLC) named Jackson head of its "Operation Breadbasket" in Chicago. The operation was designed to bring bread and income into the homes of black and poor people. Jackson won an impressive list of agreements with Chicago corporations to hire and assist blacks. He worked with the SCLC throughout the civil rights movement. In 1968, the year he was ordained a Baptist minister, Jackson was with Dr. King in Memphis when King was fatally shot.

Following a split with the SCLC in 1971, Jackson founded Operation PUSH, People United to Serve Humanity; he is national president of the program. In 1975 he mobilized the PUSH for Excellence, or Project EXCEL, a self-help program which encourages students to strive for academic excellence, and calls for cooperation among students, parents, and teachers.

Jackson is a tough, quick-witted leader, an excellent fund-raiser, and a fiery, persuasive public speaker. The recipient of more than twenty-five honorary doctorates, he is associate pastor of Chicago's Fellowship Baptist Church, writes a syndicated newspaper column, and has been a visiting professor at the University of Southern California.

INTERVIEW
JESSE JACKSON

ARTHUR THOMAS: Reverend Jackson, what is the EXCEL Proposition?

JESSE JACKSON: A PUSH for Excellence is a challenge for us to develop academic and character excellence. Because we are fighting against the odds trying to survive, we cannot afford to hang around in the Martian meadows of mediocrity. Jackie Robinson was finally able to make it because he was superior, because he was excellent. Ali survived against great odds because he was excellent. Lena Horne survived against great odds, and Dr. King and Dr. Bunche achieved great things. This was their legacy to us, because they were excellent.

During this period with the job market getting tighter and universities closing down, with cybernetics taking our present jobs and with new world markets displacing us as consumers, our only protection against genocide is to remain necessary, to excel.

THOMAS: Why do you say part of the EXCEL philosophy deals with blaming the victim?

JACKSON: Because the victim has the responsibility to resist the pressure. The victim has the responsibility to avoid being tricked and further deceived. The victim has the responsibility to resist drugs and alcohol abuse. The victim has the responsibility to resist making a bad matter worse.

In this dialectic between the victim and the victimizer, the victim is not responsible for being down, but the victim must be responsible for getting up. To understand the victimizer is to know that the emphasis and the impetus must come from the victim. In other words, we got a Public Accommodations Bill because we asserted ourselves, not because of something the victimizer did. We got a Voting Rights Bill because we asserted ourselves.* There has never been a case where a victimizer or a slavemaster took a group of slaves and tied them and whipped them and beat them until they became doctors and lawyers and scientists and financiers. Entering those professions is always the agenda of free people.

THOMAS: I've heard you speak on several occasions, and I've noticed that the press always picks up the part of your speech that deals with the importance of discipline, the importance of reading and writing. But every time I've heard you speak, you also deal with the importance of changing the system. Don't you think sometimes you're accused of not dealing with the total issue simply because, although you're dealing with it, the press isn't picking up that part?

JACKSON: The issue of discipline has universal appeal. The maximum number of readers and listeners and watchers know that discipline is important, whether you're on the farm or you're in the city, whether you're black or white or brown, male or female. If you are a business person you know that discipline is important to productivity. If you are an academic person, you know that discipline is important to academic development. If you are a coach, you know that discipline is important if you're trying to win. If you are a parent, you know that discipline will save your child from some form of juvenile delinquency.

So the issue of having discipline has great appeal. Our contention is that discipline must emanate from moral authority rather than military authority. In other words, one should not be disciplined because of a threat of death or the

---

*The Public Accommodations Bill of 1964 prohibits discrimination or segregation in public facilities, public education, and federally assisted programs. It established equal employment opportunities. The Voting Rights Act of 1965 states that race, color, or previous conditions cannot affect a person's right to vote, and guarantees uniform standards for voting qualifications.

threat of jail. One should become disciplined and appreciate the significance of it. If you are going to run for the Olympics to get a gold medal, you must run, and train, and discipline yourself, not because somebody's going to shoot you, but because your competition is going to defeat you. Do you see?

I think oftentimes the media does take a lot of statements out of context, and therefore people cannot appreciate all of what one is saying. We must change the system, but those of us who are victimized by it must be the change agents, not those who are benefiting from the system at this point.

THOMAS: What great successes have you experienced with EXCEL thus far?

JACKSON: The greatest success is watching a generation of young people respond to a challenge that the broader society told us they could not respond to. We take the position that our children *can* learn. That's an interesting position to establist, that we can learn. That it's possible. Second, we *ought* to learn. It is the moral thing to do. Third, we *must* learn. It is imperative.

The revival of parental involvement makes all that possible. In a real sense, when parents aren't involved, our schools exist in isolation. Parents should do just four simple things: meet their child's teacher, and exchange home numbers; number their children's study hours at least two hours a night with television and radio off; pick up their child's test score—we shouldn't be complaining that a child's reading at the seventh grade level in the twelfth grade, we ought to know in the eighth grade if our child's reading at the seventh grade level—and lastly, pick up our child's report cards four times a year. If parents do these four things, that parent-teacher foundation will make teachers more accountable by definition, and will make students more accountable and feel that they are in a situation where somebody cares.

THOMAS : The PUSH for Excellence involves areas other than the education arena. One of your staff members said you had a meeting where oceanographers were introduced, and geneticists were introduced, and the person who got the greatest response was a disc jockey, and therefore you had to build a PUSH for Excellence strategy with the disc jockeys because they had the young people's minds.

JACKSON : Disc jockeys, professional athletes, entertainers, our radio and television personalities, educators—whoever impacts the mind is an educator to the mind. This is the first generation that by the age of fifteen has seen 18,000 hours of television, and heard more radio than that, compared with 11,000 hours of school and less than 3,000 hours of church. This means that quantitatively, the media has more access to our minds, and qualitatively its impact is greater than home, school, and church combined. By age twenty the only thing we do more than watch the media is sleep.

That's a tremendous amount of media leverage and media input. If it feeds into our minds just slick ways to make a living, slick ways to kill, slick ways to get a thrill, then we've become a slick generation as opposed to a sacrificial and meaningful generation. That's why we must literally compete for our children's minds, and then win.

We want to fight for excellence. There are some things that are impediments to excellence. Racial division, moral degeneracy and decadence, and mass media addiction are diversions. You've got the degeneracy that comes from permissiveness and moral collapse. Children are wiped out on marijuana, angel dust, cocaine, liquor, cigarettes, and the like, which affect them emotionally and physically. So to talk about pushing for academic excellence, one must also deal with those economic and social forces that serve to impede them. You've really got to keep pushing.

THOMAS : Is there anywhere in the EXCEL program a strategy designed to attack or approach the way black people treat each other—the way the black man treats the black woman, the way the black woman treats the black man, the way we move as a family unit?

JACKSON: The most fundamental step in the approach is a step called "I Am Somebody." If you really are secure in the fact that you are somebody, then you will treat yourself as if you're somebody. You will have self-respect. And one of the things self-respect obligates you to do is respect other people. Self-esteem is basic because it can be contagious. If you respect yourself, you can respect me.

In one sense, there is nothing more insecure than an underachiever, one who has not achieved his or her potential and therefore is full of guilt and insecurity. These people are forever putting their underachievement complexes onto other people. They become cynical, saying, "You don't amount to much." They have lost confidence in themselves and their saying they don't have confidence in you is nothing but projection. Or they become pessimistic, saying, "Well, there's a possibility you might make it, but there's a strong possibility you might not make it." They try to lift up the disadvantage side of every issue. We simply have to have enough self-esteem to move beyond fundamentally disrespecting people. We must learn to really judge people according to their character and contributions and not according to their color or their sex. If you are sick, you want a doctor who can heal you. The doctor's origin, age, or sex doesn't matter. If you are in trouble, you want to be freed, liberated, exonerated. The lawyer with the best logic and the most preparation is the lawyer you finally want.

I think it's at that level. Just as we are concerned about ethnicity, we also must be concerned about ethics and we must be concerned about excellence. We are talking about being ethnic, being ethical, and being excellent.

THOMAS: On a more specific level, what are your views on getting black men to learn to respect black women?

JACKSON: Black men have been struggling for too long as the object of castration. We were made to be boys downtown and couldn't even be men at home. Black women, at their highest and most mature state, in some sense protected their husbands much the way they protected their children and gave black men a sense of self-esteem, a sense of belonging, a sense of being somebody.

The mature black woman knows it is important that she preserve not only her career, but also that she preserve her family. If she loses her family, she's already lost her career. In terms of priority, we must first build our family. If our families are stable, then we can have careers and independence. But if our families collapse, we can't even reproduce. And if we can't reproduce, we can't rear our children.

This new notion of a husband and a wife being in competition as opposed to being in cooperation is a step backward. The question centers on identity. My identity is caught up in my wife and in my five children, because I must be measured, not by how _fast_ I got across the finish line, but by whether or not I pulled a wagon across the finish line with them in it. It's not so hard for me to get across the finish line like a track star. But for me to get across the finish line pulling my wife and five children means I'm a man, not because I made a baby, but because I had the patience to raise a family. You become a man or a woman by some functional definition. To produce, to protect, and to provide is a realistic kind of measurement.

Some people try to identify relationships based upon a false sense of equality. The beauty of marriage is that we lose some of the first person and the second person and become a third person. When you fuse and become one, the notion of fifty-fifty becomes ridiculous. Because you are now talking about a oneness of person, a oneness of goals, you're not hung up on sameness of roles. So I do whatever is necessary to satisfy my wife. It's not, "I did this for you, you do this for me." It's get up early in the morning, it's work late at night,

Jesse Jackson (center) holds his daughter on his shoulders during a march to protest cuts in government programs (May, 1980). Washington, D.C. (*Wide World Photos*)

it's play, it's be serious, it's provide. It's a marriage. It's a family.

THOMAS: You've been very active in foreign policy. You've visited the Middle East and Africa. What role do you think blacks play in foreign policy? How involved are we now, and how involved can we be?

JACKSON: Blacks have not been very involved in international politics. We have just now begun to be invited to the State Department to discuss Africa. We had a meeting at the State Department last week. It was one of the very few meetings that they had to discuss Africa, and then they mostly talked to us, they didn't listen to what we had to say. Now, if they think we shouldn't relate to Africa, you know they wouldn't appreciate our need to relate to other countries. For so long, foreign affairs was considered none of the slaves' business. This is a part of the legacy of slavery.

That's why we must fight to be people in the world, not just black people, but people in the world who are black. I resent anybody referring to me as a "black" leader. I am a leader who is black, and Baptist, and a bunch of other things. Now why do I resist that box? Because I do not want my ideas to be curtailed and limited by a label.

I say that children who begin to smoke cigarettes in their formative years will not grow to their proper height, and will develop heart problems, and will develop cancer and die. Educators say it, moral leaders say it, and I'm saying it to whoever will catch cancer from cigarettes—and that's whoever smokes them.

If a leader says, "Don't put dope in veins, put hope in brains," that's not just a black leader talking to black people. Whoever puts heroin in the arm will end up dead of an overdose.

No one refers to Wallace as a "white" governor, or calls Carter a "white" president. Why? Because by definition that would limit their domain; it would limit their scope. It would put a label on their ideas. You take for granted that Carter's white when you look at him or listen to him. You can take for granted that I'm black when you look at or listen to me, but don't limit me in any box.

Yes, I want to know a whole lot about foreign affairs. People with ideas must struggle and remain curious, and break out of boxes. We must relate to other countries. Take, for example, our relations with China and the Far East. The implications of this country relating to China are tremendous for the American consumer and for the American laborer. We've lost thousands of steelworkers' jobs over the last ten years. Those jobs didn't go to the ghetto on Affirmative Action as some whites think; those jobs went to Japan. We lost thousands of textile workers' jobs. Those jobs didn't go to Harlem; those jobs went to the Pacific rim. The American worker and the American consumer, across racial lines, must raise grave questions and must understand fully the implications of our economic expansion program.

THOMAS: You have visited South Africa, where the apartheid system segregates blacks and whites, where whites control the government and blacks are noncitizens. You have strong feelings on our role there. This came out recently in your involvement in the case of a South African youngster who was maimed by a white man. Could you tell us about this?

JACKSON: We have three options relative to South Africa. We can ignore South Africa, which we cannot reconcile with being humane people. We can embrace South Africa, which we cannot do and be a leader of the free world. Or we can use economic leverage and fight South Africa to limit South African cultural expression and economic expansion.

In the instance you're asking about, Kallie Knoetse, a boxer and a South African policeman, shot a child twice in the back of the legs. This fifteen-year-old boy had to have his leg amputated. Worse than that, not only did Knoetse shoot the boy twice, he then brought charges against the African boy for provoking him to shoot him. The boy didn't charge

Knoetse with the shooting; it's hard for a black noncitizen in South Africa to charge an officer of the state with a crime. The boy finally won the case to keep from going to jail with his one leg. The boxer later beat up two witnesses who were about to testify in a case involving another policeman. It was not a felony in South Africa, it was a misdemeanor, but it was a felony when translated into American judicial standards.

Knoetse was scheduled for a boxing match in Madison Square Garden. We challenged Madison Square Garden not to sponsor the event. They said it was up to CBS. We challenged CBS. They collaborated to put on the event. As a matter of fact, it was their money that made the fight go.

We picketed that event. More importantly, we got the State Department for the first time to declare a strong position on South African expansion. They revoked Knoetse's visa. A judge, through a temporary restraining order, protected his staying here. He's tied up in court right now. We are going to get him deported. Most important, on the day that he fought, because of the international pressure that we were able to bring to bear, they desegregated boxing in South Africa, and they are now going to desegregate the arena where people sit at boxing matches. That's only because we grabbed a significant issue at the critical moment, and held onto it until some change came.

When we fight, we may not make all the progress that we seek, but if we do not fight, we are guaranteed to go backward.

THOMAS: Reverend Jackson, thank you from the bottom of our hearts for hanging in there, for not giving up the fight. Keep on doing what you're doing for the people. Thank you very much for "Like It Is."

JACKSON: Thank you for working me to death. That's the way it really is!

February 23, 1979

PHOTOGRAPH CREDITS: *Page 1*, Gerard W. Purcell Associates, Ltd.; *page 17*, Wide World Photos; *page 55*, Wide World Photos; *page 101*, Carol Geddes; *page 115*, Greg Stewart; *page 129*, Wide World Photos.